The ICE OPINION

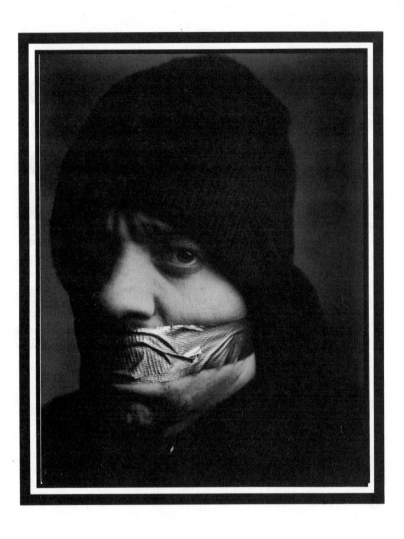

The ICE OPINION

who gives a FUCK?

ICE T

as told to Heidi Siegmund

St. Martin's Press ∎ New York

Photographs of Ice T © Mark Seliger. Used by permission.
Design by Sara Stemen
Album cover art on page 182 © David Halili.

Library of Congress Cataloging-in-Publication Data
Ice T (Musician)
    The Ice Opinion / Ice T as told to Heidi Siegmund.
        p.   cm,
    ISBN 0-312-10486-3
    1. Ice T (Musician)—Interviews.   2. Rap musicians—United States—Interviews.
    I. Siegmund, Heidi.   II. Title.
    ML420.I3A5   1994
    782.42164—dc20   93-40361
                                                            CIP
                                                            MN

First Edition: February 1994
10   9   8   7   6   5   4   3   2   1

Contents

Preface

I've managed to sum up my experiences as a rap artist in one word: interpretation. No two people process information the same way. They interpret information by funneling it through the agendas in their own heads. *The Ice Opinion: Who Gives a Fuck?* lets you in on the agenda in my head, in words that should be easily understood even by the average high school dropout.

I didn't write this book to make you like me, though I hope you do. I wrote *The Ice Opinion* in an attempt to inspire conversation. I hope the subjects I address in this book will provoke other people to state their opinions, no matter how farfetched they might seem. I subtitled the book *Who Gives a Fuck?* to keep people from taking anything I say as the word of God, or, depending on your interpretation, the word of the Antichrist. Anything that comes out of my mouth could be totally wrong, but this is how I see the world around me.

This is not a biography; I have no interest in books that smack of self-importance. This does not mean that the issues I discuss do not matter to me. I care deeply about everything from crime to sex, I just don't expect anyone else to care.

Throughout my career I've given numerous in-depth interviews, and this book represents one-stop shopping for anybody who wants to document what's on my mind. My opinions have changed during the ten years I've been in the public eye, and this will give me a chance to update and clarify where I'm coming from and where I've been.

Fortunately, I've seen things the way a lot of other people have seen them, and I know there are enough of you out there who will read this and understand that we're all not really that different.

Part I
WHO GIVES
A FUCK?

1 The Jungle Creed

"**W**ho gives a fuck?" is one of the first questions a kid will ask himself growing up in the ghetto. He'll look around at the broken-down buildings, the shabby projects, the cracked schoolyard playgrounds, and it doesn't look like anybody gives a fuck. He'll watch mean muthafuckas in patrol cars rolling around the neighborhood, and they won't give a fuck. Everybody he sees is just trying to survive; they are just trying to make it over to another day.

This is his view from there. To understand where the rage and defiance in inner-city kids come from, you have to understand the attitude of people when they're down. Even a strong-willed kid will have a difficult time giving a fuck when everywhere he looks, the cops, the schools, and the people outside of the ghetto reinforce his feelings of helplessness.

The ghetto is the compiled interest of lost hope.

ORIGINAL GANGSTER ■ Ten years ago I used to listen to rappers flow,

When you're down in that hole, you have a real different view of right and wrong.

In the ghetto, the cop is the dog catcher. Once he's got his net on you, you're gone. You have no way out. So when you see him, you're immediately scared because if he's the dog catcher, you're the dog. So hide from him, bite him, shoot him, but don't even think you're going to have a conversation with him.

Throughout the history of America, the police have never been friends to black people. When we came over here on the slave ships, the police were the people with the whips, the ones who got paid to keep us in line. They were the guards at every plantation, who hunted us down when we ran away and humiliated us at the stocks once they found us. There has never been a black leader in the history of America who's been a friend to the police. No black leader ever said, "Honor the cops"—unless he was a cop.

So, when teachers or politicians tell black kids to respect the police, the kids are thinking, "Why? Where do I get that from? Where's my role model?" You have to analyze the law enforcement's treatment of black people. Before anybody's ever gonna respect the police they have to respect the judicial system first. You have to believe it isn't a big vacuum cleaner that sweeps us up. You have to understand that the judicial system is a no-win situation for minorities.

When you're coming out of the ghetto you learn the cops aren't your friends, and you quickly realize they are the enemy. Very seldom do you see them come and do anything outside of pulling people out of the ghetto for something. You always see them picking up brothers. Cops don't walk up to people in the ghetto, especially members of the Los Angeles Police Department, and say, "Hi. How are you doing?" The first time a cop ever treated me like a human

■ Talkin' 'bout the way they rocked the mic at the disco.

4

being was when I got a gig rapping in the film *Breakin'*. But before that, the only time I ever saw them was when they were coming after somebody. In poor environments, there is a lot of crime because people are so desperate. The criminal mentality is reinforced by the way the police in the ghetto treat you. When you're down there and you got the cops cruising around looking at you like you're already guilty, it just multiplies your feelings of worthlessness.

Anybody in the ghetto can tell you the cops aren't there to "protect and serve" them. You don't have to wait to hear about it, you learn by experience. One night, my buddy's mother called the police because her car radio had gotten stolen. My buddies and I were standing out in front of her house when the cops pulled up onto her front lawn. They got out of the patrol car and screamed at us to spread out on the grass. His mom came running out of the house crying, "That's my son." The cops waved their guns at her and yelled, "Shut up. Go in the house."

They searched us, shook us down, asked us if we were in a gang and all this kind of drag, and then they told us to leave. After we scattered, they went up to the front door and listened to her story. She explained that somebody had broken into her car and stolen her radio. The cops told her, "It was probably one of your sons. They looked like they were on drugs. You know, this is the neighborhood."

There was no report. No reassurance. No nothing. They were basically saying to her, "Don't call us around here for no car radio." I'll never forget that incident. I kept thinking "What are police fuckin' here for?" After a while, you see them and you just wonder, "What are they gonna do with me now?" You get real accustomed to that attitude.

In Los Angeles, the LAPD has little tricks up their sleeve to help get you in their system, and they use them very effectively. Their key specialty is the Los Angeles jaywalking/

■ I liked how that shit was goin' down,
■ Dreamed about rippin' the mic with my own sound.

traffic ticket warrant. You can be the squarest kid on the street, but then you'll get a jaywalking or a traffic ticket you can't afford to pay. How you gonna get $250 to pay a traffic ticket that can immediately turn into a bench warrant? So the next time they stop you, they catch you with a warrant and you go to jail. This turns a kid who ain't done nothing into a criminal. Immediately, they snatch you up into their system.

In my old neighborhood, the LAPD's objective was to pop every kid on the street. If you lived in a different neighborhood, maybe this tactic wouldn't be so detrimental. Maybe your mother might have $250 to pay the ticket, and it might be nothing.

But you got to remember a lot of people in the ghetto might pay $250 for rent. And if your mom is on welfare, you're living off $8,000 a year or less. And that's not all cash, that's food stamps, too. So, just try to understand that something as simple as a parking ticket can send you under. Within the system, there's no way of working it off. There's no way of saying, "Can I get out of it?"

It's widely known the cops use this tool to get you on the books in their system. Until you get a ticket, until they mess with you, they don't have any adult fingerprints on you. Sometimes, cops will even take you into jail and print you because you "fit a description." That's a commonly used phrase that basically means they can fuck with you. You might be walking down the street and before you know it, you're getting printed. They're on a mission in the ghetto to print entire neighborhoods. They make you out as a criminal before you even know what's going on. Eventually, they're gonna book everybody for something or other and get you into that jail system.

The treatment of people in the 'hood by the LAPD contributes to your feelings of inferiority. The people who are in this position down there feel like they are unwelcome anywhere else. If you're driving through Bel Air and you're stopped by the LAPD, they'll look at your zip code or run your license number through their computers and determine where you're living. If you're living at 96th and Western, you'll hear, "Get out and lay down!" If your zip code shows Beverly Hills then it's a totally different routine. The people in the 'hood get treated in a way that nobody else gets treated. They know economically you can't fight back. And if you do, you usually lose. Since 1986, 47,000 accusations of police brutality were filed with the U.S. Justice Department and only sixty of the attackers were prosecuted.

If nothing else, you don't like it when you see a cop coming; but until you live in the ghetto, you just can't understand.

The ghetto is set up like a concentration camp. The government has broken the system down to a series of financially segregated villages. South Central is not a black community, it's a poor community. You live there 'cause you're broke, not because you're black.

I knew a free-lance writer from Denmark who moved down to Vernon and Broadway because he was sent over here with only $500 a month. Until he got some other work, he was gonna be totally broke. Now, this is a blond-haired, blue-eyed guy living in the 'hood.

At first, people in the neighborhood would whisper, "Who's that white boy?" After a while, he became known as "the white boy." A little while later, he became "the white dude." And after two years, he finally made it to "homeboy" status. Now, everybody loves him. Everybody knows him. This dude talks like me, he totally picked up the whole attitude. He'll tell me that when he first came to town, he couldn't get a place to live cheaper than his apartment in

■ **My boys said, "That ain't you Ice, that shit sounds like them."**

South Central. He couldn't get near Hollywood, no West L.A., no Valley. He was stuck. But after a while, he started to dig the neighborhood. He felt like a foreign war correspondent.

Why does it take somebody from out of the country to make that step? What would white Americans do if they became that broke? What would happen if all of a sudden a whole bunch of white people hit it real hard and ended up on welfare? I don't know what they would do. They'd probably lose their minds. I don't think they'd move to South Central or live apart from each other. I don't know how the government would create a place for them to live, but I'm sure they would probably come up with something.

The funny thing is, the ghetto would welcome them because the nature of black people is very loving. The nature of anybody who's down is very generous. They are the first to invite you to come into their house and let them feed you. So if you ain't from there and you're down on your luck, you'll most likely be welcomed by the people. They just don't want to be judged.

Early on, kids growing up in the inner city learn in school there ain't no reason to go to college 'cause they ain't getting a decent job anyway. I don't know where that comes from, but it's there, and when you're there, it deeply affects you. It may be a big hoax, but you never forget it.

The successful people you see in the ghetto are the drug dealers, the pimps—the brothers driving around in the flashy cars. Your role models are these fly guys because everybody else is struggling. The hustlers look like they got it going on. You don't really see them do dirt. They pay someone else to handle their business. You just see their accumulation of wealth, and it's more than you got, so you're naturally attracted to them and their lifestyle.

■ So I sat back, thought up a new track
■ Didn't fantasize, kicked the pure facts.

8

The only reason you see the drug dealers always driving through your streets is they have to get paid. Most of them don't live there anymore, but they have to come back to the neighborhood to make the money. They leave because they can't stay down there in an environment where people know who's got the money and who doesn't.

In *Pimp: The Story of My Life,* Iceberg Slim wrote, "The jungle creed says the strong must feed on any prey at hand." If you're in a poor environment and you're a doctor, people may say to you, "Hey, brother, you made it. Congratulations." But the jungle creed says you can't just stay there, because if you get your money up, eventually the poor people around you are gonna have to prey.

It's gonna happen, even though they may not want it to happen. The whole neighborhood can be down with Dr. John, the man who lives on the street and made it to the other side. But another guy's living across the street—broke, on drugs— and he becomes the predator. He's looking up and down the street and everybody's broke, but there's that one house with a nice lawn and a new paint job. The owner's probably got a bit of money, he's thinking. That dude's gonna have to come get you 'cause he can't see any other way out. So sooner or later, Dr. John has got to leave the neighborhood. He's looking like a big piggy bank sitting in the middle of despair, and that ain't no place to be.

In the ghetto, you're constantly living in a survivalist atmosphere. All these people are on top of each other, pushing and scrambling all in an attempt to get out of this hole. Everyone is trying to survive and in this microcosm of people, you might see a guy who appears a little richer, but basically everybody's broke. It's difficult to teach basic moral principles like charity and loaning and trust. The environment is also

■ Muthafuckas got scared, cause they was unprepared,

poisoned with drugs, so a lot of people there aren't really even themselves.

In the jungle, masculinity is at a premium. Anybody weaker than the next man will be victimized by the stronger. You learn early on—like in grade school—if I'm weak and you're stronger, when I go over and buy my ice cream sandwich, you're gonna reach over and break off half. That's how you live and you get used to it. It's the animal instinct.

The white knight is not the hero. Displays of strength and aggression are prized because you're always walking like a prison inmate. In the 'hood, violence and even murder become something honorable. The most violent person, the most defiant person, will get the highest ranking. The person who pushes it to the limit and is willing to go to jail earns the most props because he's willing to put his life on the line to fight for what he believes in.

Once you're down there, you've got this walk, this attitude, that says "Don't fuck with me." You don't understand anybody who is weak. You look at gay people as prey. There isn't anybody in the ghetto teaching that some people's sexual preferences are predisposed. You're just ignorant. You got to get educated, you got to get out of that jail cell called the ghetto to really begin to understand. All you see is a sissy. A soft dude. A punk.

That's how it is when you're down there. Everybody walks around looking at each other crazy. That's why you find that girls who live in the neighborhood are so tough. I don't care how pretty they are, each one of them has a real strong side to her just to survive.

When there's less of anything, the stronger people get more. If there's a party and six Beverly Hills kids wanted to go in a car that only sat four, the four most popular kids would get in that car and the others would leave. In the ghetto,

■ **Who would tell it like it really was? Who dared?**

the strongest kids would get in that car. The other two couldn't or wouldn't come near it.

Your ranking system ain't based on what you got because you ain't got nothing. It's based on who you are. Now, the whole idea of who you are comes from what little you got and how resourceful you are at making it into something. That's why you see all those sneakers when you go to New York City. You'll never see so many sneaker stores anywhere else. Why? Because the kids don't have cars, so their cars are their sneakers.

You may wonder why black kids wash their sneakers. Because that's all they got. This is how they are being judged among their peers. They are being judged by what model sneakers they got or by their little gold chains. If you're going home to a project and you don't own anything, and neither does the next guy, you take pride in your gold chain. Your whole self-esteem is based on making something special out of the little you might have.

You get respect by how you dress and how you carry yourself. When we see white kids or rich kids dress like bums, we never understand it. Why the fuck would they *try* to look like that? We're over here pressing our fucking jeans every day, and it may be the one pair of jeans we got.

I've come to believe a lot of people's appearances reflect their search for the opposite. That's why Bon Jovi will try to look bummy, and why I'm not trying to look bummy. I used to *have* to look like a bum, because that was all I had.

The funny thing about the ghetto is when you're living there, you don't even know you're there. You don't have anything to compare it to. Everything you see on TV, you think it's not real.

If you're not traveling out of an area, your scope is so

■ A muthafucka from the West Coast, L.A.,
■ South Central fool, where the Crips and Bloods play.

limited. I grew up in a New Jersey ghetto, and when I first moved to Los Angeles, I lived in Windsor Hills. Windsor Hills may be a nice black neighborhood, but I thought I was in Beverly Hills. I didn't know that as far as the rest of L.A. was concerned, Windsor Hills was still considered the ghetto. In other words, Windsor Hills is nice, but the top-of-the-line house up there is only $300,000.

The first time I took some of my boys from the 40s into Beverly Hills and Bel Air, when we drove past some of the homes, they asked me some ill questions:

"Is that an apartment building?"

"How many people live in there?"

"How many houses is that really?"

They couldn't believe it could possibly be one house.

I'll never forget the illest comment. It came from my buddy's brother, Bebop Bill. Looking up at one mansion he said, "Imagine what they eat."

He was thinking about food! He said dreamily, "They can probably eat whatever they want to." He's really saying, "I don't eat what I want to eat. I eat what I can eat."

When you grow up and live in South Central, just having a job and making ends meet is a luxury. We fail to realize that just the thought of eating what you want to for dinner is a treat. Just to be able to say, "Yo, I'd like to eat a steak tonight," and then go to the market, pick one up and eat it— that's a luxury. To have a roof over your head and to eat what you want is the ultimate. It comes down to your taste buds, man.

If you're working with $1.40 and that's all you got, you have to fabricate meals. It's not like you can eat what you want to eat. When you're poor broke, you head for McDonald's and think to yourself, "Damn, if I don't get the cheese and if I get a small Coke, I can do this." I've been in situations where we've been in the crib, and there's been no

■ **When I wrote about parties it didn't fit,**

12

money between four people and everybody's bumming, "Damn, we ain't got no milk. We got shit that don't add up, like Kool-Aid and no sugar and oatmeal." You start making scientific food and cooking without grease. You ain't got the right ingredients. You're just thinking, "What the fuck are we gonna eat?" If you go home, there ain't no food there 'cause Moms is broke. In the ghetto your parents often won't have any money, and they'll almost tell you, "Do what you got to do."

Kids end up hustling and stealing because they ain't got nothing there. It gets bad. And no matter what the reason for the poverty or the situation that put people in poverty, the problem is it exists. People ain't got no money. When you're in that situation, your perception of what's right is so totally different than someone who grows up in a middle-class neighborhood.

Ghetto kids grow up in this fucked-up world, and they think that's how it is and they can't do anything about it. Until you get up and out of it, people don't see that there are any alternatives. They don't know anything about the community I live in now. They are so far away from it. All of my neighbors currently are preparing to die of old age. They've got their life insurance policies all in order and their wills are written up. You go to my old neighborhood and just try to talk about retirement plans. The mentality is, "Retirement? I'm just worried about living till next year. I don't know what you're talking about." The greatest tragedy in the ghetto is watching people become accustomed to the prospect of a bleak future. If you try to talk to them about a positive future, you'll learn they don't really see no future. It's too dim, too untouchable.

The ghetto mentality forces you to become very resilient. It teaches you to be able to handle anything that comes your

■ **"Six 'n the Morning," That was the real shit."**

way. The greatest danger with that is you become so branded and you allow people on the outside of the ghetto to try to make you feel uncomfortable when you're not there.

I try so hard to explain to kids who I meet that when you actually venture outside of your 'hood, there is nothing out there that is not yours. I don't want them believing that their neighborhood is all they got. Why can't you go surfing? Who says surfing is just for white kids? That's your wave, too. That's your snow mountain up there in Big Bear. Let's go skiing. Let's go horseback riding. Let's go jet skiing. Everything is everybody's.

But you see, each time you go to one of those places I mentioned, you're gonna have eyes rolling at you. "What are *they* doing here? Why are *they* trying to play golf? Why aren't *they* where they're supposed to be?" A lot of kids just find it less frustrating to just stay where they are. The ghetto may be a hard, very strange place, but no one's judging you for being there. At the core of it, there's a lot of family love in the ghetto you don't feel other places. The ghetto has its own vibe, its own attitude. If you go to Harlem, people will tell you, "We're all down. We're all trying to hustle, but we're all together here."

In South Central, however, there's a lot of bitterness and a lot of misguided people and it all stems from ignorance. The school system there does nothing to help. The curriculum that is offered in ghetto schools only reinforces the high dropout rate among these kids.

You're given books to read and to learn from about shit that just seems so farfetched from what you are and what you know and how you live. If you came home at the end of each school day and your father was a chemist or a doctor, algebra might begin to make sense to you then. It might make sense that you need to know algebraic equations. But when you don't know nothing like that, and you don't know any-

■ Original Gangster.
■ When I wrote about parties, someone always died.

14

thing about your own history, you just feel you're nothing. You just lose total hope. I believe that's the worst thing that can happen to you in the ghetto, to lose all hope.

The ghetto is the compiled interest of lost hope; you feel stuck there and there's no way you can see out. The only people you see making it are the kids hustling, and it's just a paradox that draws you deeper and deeper through jail and through lots of trouble.

I see the frustrations of this mind-set so clearly; I'm basically a product of it. My whole mission is to not only talk to kids about the anxieties, but to set an example by continuing to excel and by continuing to climb up. I want to be more and more of a success.

People say, "Ice T, you should rap about this or that." I don't give a fuck about what people say. The biggest role model I have is just the fact I'm achieving. Fuck what I'm rapping about. Fuck "Cop Killer." Fuck the way I dress. I want people to say, "This brother was down here with us, and now he's making something and he's attempting to tell us how to do it."

I've had so many people from the 'hood step to me and say, "Yo, when I see you do a movie, it makes me think I can do that. When I see you write a book, it means I could be writing a book." That's why I'm reaching in so many different directions. I didn't want to become somebody who could only do one thing. "Oh, this dude used to be in a gang and now he makes rap records. You know, that's all they can do is rap."

Nah. Uh-uh. I haven't worked this hard just to be pigeonholed. That's why I own my own label now, to show these kids you can do it all. That's the type of role model they need. Someone who tells them, "Sure you can hit everything." It's very important the role model shows them you

■ **When I tried to write happy, yo, I knew I lied.**

don't need to leave your black roots behind. Regardless of what you got to do, you can still be a homeboy. That's why I still look like them and run this company. Russell Simmons doesn't need to put on a suit and tie to run Def Jam. He's another brother who's out there setting an example for these kids.

Don King taught me you can walk into a meeting with your hair combed straight up in the air, and it doesn't matter. It has absolutely nothing to do with your looks, it's what you got in your head. I can come to a business meeting in a diaper, and the other businessmen will say, "Eccentric. Different. But he's got what we need."

I've watched Don King come off and say, "I'm a nigger. And I'm always gonna be a nigger." And people don't like Don King because he's like that. I believe that's one of the reasons Mike Tyson went down. Tyson was attached to Don King, and people hate Don King. You know why people hate Don King? 'Cause Don King is still a nigger. And he don't give a fuck. He'll tell you straight up that he's got $20 million and if you could have put him in jail, he'd be there by now. Fact is he ain't breaking no laws. And if you still got a problem with him, he'll tell you his books are open for inspection. And fuck you, and fuck you, he's saying. 'Cause he's about to do King Vision, a $200 million venture. Any questions? Don King is all that; he's one of my idols. I'm a true believer you can keep the same attitude once you start breaking out of the ghetto.

Those are the kinds of role models people in the ghetto need. Basically, they need to see ghetto people getting over, but not turning into something they can't be or they can't relate to. Ghetto kids don't want to be Bryant Gumbel. They can't even relate to him.

It's funny though, 'cause they still love Michael Jackson.

Michael is just so dope. Michael can make the hardest gangster sit in the front row and scream like a bitch. You can't hate Michael because everybody grew up with him, and you love every one of his songs. You might not love him for what he did to himself, but you know you've been rocking to Michael all your life. Unlike Bryant Gumbel, who just comes off like a square white wannabe.

In the future, the dominant culture will rule in America. People from the ghetto are the dominant culture. That's why you're seeing a lot of shit change. You're seeing very hip white people. You're seeing kids just getting stronger and more militant and radical on all fronts. They ain't teaching you any of this in school. It's coming out of the 'hood.

People are comparing notes, which is important. If you're somebody who grew up in a suburb and went to college, but you have no idea how to throw a punch or defend yourself, you're gonna need to learn. By the same token, kids from the ghetto need to learn how to be less aggressive and how to solve more of their problems with their brains.

I want these kids to know the skills they learn *on* the street are as valuable as the skills they learn *off* the street. The person who can merge both of them together the quickest will be the achiever. Kids from the ghetto need to step back and realize, "Okay, I've been to one college, and now I'm gonna search for the other side." With that mind-set, you can conquer any goal you want. I've learned that most everything you do in business can be traced back to something you learned on the street. So value it.

I run into people all the time in the music industry who don't have any street sense. The smart ones quickly hire somebody who does. They understand they are going to need somebody to back them and connect them into that world.

■ A simple look and anyone with two cents would know

That's why I gave a speech at Time Warner for all the executives. They know they have this big hole in their head when it comes to the ghetto.

"What do you mean by 'dope'?" they'll ask. I know they feel ignorant because it's a world they are so far removed from. Now that I'm running my own company, I'm in a search to learn what they know. So it works both ways.

I want kids to understand that the ghettos they were raised in may be thought of as negative, but they are gonna need to be tough in life and in business. To get into business, you'll need tact and courage because you're gonna be taking risks. If you're from the 'hood, you've already got an advantage—you've probably been hustling and battling on a different scale and by the time you're sitting around the executive table, it's not a big thing. It usually requires no different skills than those you may have learned dealing drugs. The people in the meeting will be sweating and tripping. You'll be sizing them up, and they'll be sizing you up, and offers get made and terms are agreed upon and then you're out of there.

Once you establish that desire in the ghetto kid to want to go out and learn the advantages that college kids have, society has got to step in and allow them that chance. The outside has to allow and welcome them in. We've got to give them an opportunity, too. If you want to do this in the form of loans, give them loans. If you don't think they are smart enough to handle the money, give them school vouchers, but don't let a good education just be another luxury of the rich.

If you're always gonna have a group of poor people over here on one side, you're always gonna have a problem. Because you've basically got a powder keg of people who are gonna lash out any minute at who they think are the rich or are taking advantage of them. So it's entirely up to you. You can either pay them now or pay later.

The solutions all seem so clear to me, so what's the

fuckin' problem? Is it just a problem of people not wanting somebody else to have something? Is that the problem? You just don't want me to have something? Even though it seems so simple to change the rules. It seems so logical to set up the game and allow other people to get into business and have opportunities to run their own corporations and organizations. If you don't want me to compete, if you want to keep this off-sided game going—if *that's* what it is—then you have to prepare for whatever happens and whatever this game evolves into.

In order to break down the gates of the ghetto, we cannot allow the ghetto to confine us—mentally or physically. I'm thrilled to be able to move out into the hills and away from the jungle, because every other day my next-door neighbor steps out of his house and gripes, "Niggers on the left of me, Jews on the right of me." Man, this is like Christmas to me. I'm very happy to be annoying my neighbor. Do you understand?

His attitude is, "Let me pay you to go back home. Go back to the place you came from. Go back to Africa." And I tell him, "No. Because I'm from earth, muthafucka. And if I want to live anywhere, I'll live there. There is no 'place' for me." I'm as American as he is. Where am I supposed to be? Back in the 'hood, standing on the corner drinking a 40? I'm not supposed to be able to afford a nicer house than his in Beverly Hills. I'm not supposed to be seen dining in Chasen's. Fuck that. If people are going to try to make you feel out of place in any other environment than the ghetto, fuck that. Go to Chasen's and look crazy at everybody, you dig what I'm saying? My whole attitude is, I'd love to be able to buy my buddies a house up here. I'd love to be able to buy ten houses up here and turn this into my community. Who says it's theirs? Who the fuck are they?

■ **Rappin' bout hardcore topics over hardcore drum beats.**

■ ■ ■

I think the ghetto attitude can change but people have to want to get out and realize there are no real walls around them keeping them in. You can grow up in Harlem, but there's nothing wrong with moving to Central Park West.

It's extremely difficult, however, for anyone to make that step out. First, you have to mentally escape the killing fields. You have to mentally want to leave the ghetto. You can begin your escape by understanding that somebody outside of the ghetto invented the theory that once you get over, you shouldn't leave. "You should stay in the ghetto, 'cause that's where you belong." Man, the only reason you live there is because your mama's poor. Your mama lives off $400 a month, and you get what's left. People would be living in Malibu if they could afford to. You don't choose the ghetto. Everybody would like to be surrounded by beauty and would like to feel safe in their homes.

I want to explain to people that when they do get over the wall, *leave*, but come back and pick up your friends. Give them a chance to make a better life for themselves, too. Invest your money there by helping your own people, by giving them an opportunity to branch out. I've got about thirty homies on my payroll, and I do everything I can to keep them on the street and out of the prison system and away from the violence. I'm probably the biggest bail bondsman on the West Coast. My point is you can help each other get a leg up.

The whole theory is to tear down this one big Indian reservation called the black ghetto. The government's never gonna put that hospital in there they keep promising. They are never gonna change the police's attitude or pump in the outside money it'll take to make the place livable. It ain't coming. The situation's just gonna get worse.

I just want to try and break that whole mind-set. Once you grow up in the inner city, it's always gonna be in you.

■ **A little different than the average though,**
■ **Jet through the fast lane, drop ya on death row.**

It's not like you suddenly leave and wake up the next day acting square. Your points of reference are still going to be the same, but you'll have the opportunity to begin the breakdown of that aggressive, survivalist mentality. You finally realize not everybody is out to get you and you become more at peace with yourself and everybody else. You're not in that constant fear mode of knowing you've got one more dollar than the next guy and wondering where the next hit will come from. Outside the ghetto, it's not like everybody is victimizing each other. They might victimize each other in other ways, but by the time you leave the jungle, you can handle anything the nicer neighborhoods might dish out.

At times, I miss that edge. I feel less safe. I'm not always sweating or worrying about what's gonna happen next. On the other hand, I love the notion that my kid might have the chance to die of old age.

That's just my opinion on the jungle, who gives a fuck.

■ 'Cause anybody who's been there knows that
■ Life ain't so lovely on the blood-soaked fast track.

2 The Killing Fields

Gangs were born out of this chaos—the inner city. When you grow up in South Central, and you've never had anything in your life you control, you seek control. Gangs offer you ultimate control to do what you want. Just getting that for a minute is very intoxicating. Gang members are out there trying to control their own little world. It's only a little tiny place. It may not look like much to you—an alley, a street—but it's like a country to them. It's easy for outsiders to say it's just a little block, but a lot of those kids won't leave that block for years, and in some cases their entire lives. It's theirs. That becomes their whole world. Everybody wants to have power over their world.

I'm no authority on how gang warfare got started, but it's a real war. Lots of people don't see that. They just think it's stupid kids out there

The most dangerous black man in America is the ghetto hustler....These ghetto teenagers see the hell caught by their parents stuggling to get somewhere, or they see that they have given up struggling in the prejudiced, intolerant white man's world.... The ghetto hustler is internally restrained by nothing. He has no religion, no concept of morality, no civic responsibility, no fear—nothing.
—Malcolm X
THE AUTOBIOGRAPH
OF MALCOLM
196

■ That invincible shit don't work.

shooting at each other. If that's the case, then any war can be regarded as such.

Try to just imagine somebody in your family getting killed by a neighbor, maybe a teenager across the street. The police come to your door, take down the information, and don't do anything about it. Each day after that, you gotta look at these same people. Would you go over there and kill them?

I don't know. Maybe you would, maybe you wouldn't. There's a definite point where a feud begins. Once it starts, it's not easy to stop. You have a little baby my son's age growing up, and he'll put on clothes and somebody will step to him and say, "What is he doing wearing that red shirt?" A Blood—a guy from another gang—may have killed this guy's uncle. So because of this, your kid grows up in the 'hood not wearing a red T-shirt.

I've literally had friends come to my house and question what my baby boy, Ice, was wearing. "Why you putting him in this color? Why he wearing that?" I tell them, "Nigga, Ice ain't tripping with that." And they'll say, "Yeah, yeah. I'm just playing, but why don't you put him in this *blue* shirt?"

The gang scene in Los Angeles is extremely complicated and deep-rooted. The Hispanic gangs have been banging for far more years than any of the black gangs. The black gangs began to form after the Watts riots in '65, after so many brothers were thrown in jail.

I first came in contact with gangs in 1974, when I started going to Crenshaw High School. I saw this one group of guys hanging out together, and I wanted to know what was going on. They were *the* unit. At this point, I unknowingly got connected in with the Crips. When you go to school, and you start hanging out with friends from one neighborhood, this immediately becomes your gang. These guys had come from

■ **Throw ya in the joint, you'll be coming out feet first.**

Horace Mann Junior High School, and they were part of the first generation of black gangs. Across town was a gang called the Brims, which are called the Bloods now. I then started to learn all about the different groups and their idiosyncrasies.

Gang divisions are called sets. A gang member will ask you, "What set are you from?" Meaning, "Are you a Crip? Are you a Westside Crip? A Rollin' 60s Crip? Eight-Tray Gangsters? Avalon Gardens? Project Watts?"

Some of the gangs' basic characteristics are: The Crips wear blue, the Brims wear red. The Crips call you cuz. The Brims call you blood. The Crip has his left ear pierced. The Brim has his right ear pierced.

The gangbanger clothes are all based on the cheapest shit in the stores. Bandanas. Shoelaces. The Mexican kids wear pressed T-shirts; they even iron a crease in them. They wear khakis and corduroy house shoes that cost five or ten dollars. They wear Pendleton shirts that last forever. The entire dress code consists of inexpensive items, but they press them and turn their dress into something that's honorable 'cause this is all they got.

Even the lowriders were a result of kids being broke. They couldn't afford to buy a new car, so they took the car they had and turned it into a flamboyant piece of art that's theirs. They took an old '60s Chevy and put some rims on it, added a custom interior and a custom paint job and made it the coolest car in the neighborhood. When they began adding hydraulic systems, lowriding even became a sport.

In black gangs, anything that's not a Crip is a Blood. This means the Blood gangs weren't all necessarily connected. You'd have the Bounty Hunters, Pirus, Denver Lanes, Villains, Swans. But they didn't get along together, and the lack of unity made them less potent than the Crip gang.

As the gangs evolved, the Crip gangs became so wild and notorious they started to prey on themselves and divide

■ So I blast the mic with my style.

among their own sets. The Grape Street Crips in Watts would be at war with the Rollin' 60s. (The numbers, like the "60s," correspond to the street blocks. The street area where the gang activity would happen would not be too far from the west of Crenshaw Boulevard, all the way to the east as far as Long Beach Boulevard, and back into Watts. So when you hear people talk about the 20s, the "20" refers to 20th through 29th streets.)

The 30s go all the way across town, but the actual gang, the 30s, lives right around Western and the South Central police station. The 40s were the hustlers. They were the closest thing to non–gang members out of all the blocks. These were the kids who were out there gambling. They thought they were a little slicker than gang members.

Out of ten blocks, one street would be poppin' and a gang would be named after it. You had Five-Deuce (52 Hoover) Crips, Eight-Tray Crips. Before there were a Rollin' 60s and 74 Hoover—that's the hot spot of the Crip gang—they used to have a gang called 7459 Hoover Crips, which meant everything from 74th to 59th streets. And each set would have an east or a west side, like the 74 Hoover Westside or the 74 Hoover Eastside.

All these gangs have their own hand signals. A Hoover Crip would throw two fingers down and put another finger across, to look like an "H." The Crips hold up a "C." A Blood will make his fingers look like a "B." Even the hand signals are intricate. They can tell each other to fuck off from one set to another by throwing up their signals.

When a gang member gets ready for battle or goes hardcore gangbanging, they call that loc-ing. Going loc. Loc-ing up. All of a sudden the beanies will get down crazy and their pants will sag, the sunglasses are on. It's the equivalent of Native Americans going on the warpath.

I've been to parties where my homies were chillin', and

■ Sometimes I'm ill, the other times buck wild.

even though they're in a gang, they're low-key. And a fight will break out and immediately my guys go on loc. Their hats flip up and they're ready to pop. They spread the gang energy and start vibing off each other.

Even if I didn't come out and say I was in a Crip set, a gang member reading this book will naturally know because a Blood would never use the word "loc." When it became public I was involved in a Crip gang, interviewers asked me which set I was affiliated with. I still don't think it's to anybody's advantage for me to publicly represent a set. I don't want to be responsible for somebody targeting that set for any reason. You have to remember, this is no joke on the street. People live and die over their colors.

I also run into problems when I talk to Brims about the gang truce that started in April of '92. They might not want to listen to me because I'm not in their set. Bangers would feel me out first by asking what set I was with, and each time I would tell them it's irrelevant, because now I'm trying to work for everybody.

"Oh, so you was a Blood?" they'd ask.

"Fuck a Blood," I'd snap. It's an immediate response, because a lot of my friends got killed by Bloods. A lot of my friends. The last time we were on the road, one of my buddies' brother got killed in gang violence. We had to do everything we could just to keep him from retaliating, because my buddy knew who the murderer was. His brother had called 911 right before he got shot and named the killer.

And I really felt bad for my buddy, because I used to be so emotional. I would just go on autopilot, and you couldn't talk to me. That's exactly what happens to these kids. They just go crazy. When you don't retaliate, you're just sitting around waiting, waiting on justice to be served.

The question is, will he get justice? Will these guys go

■ But the science is always there.
■ I'd be a true sucker if I acted like I didn't care.

26

to jail? Will they get served? Or will he have to issue his own form of justice?

Try to put yourself in the position of losing your sister or your brother. You'd be crazy with revenge, driving around the streets asking people, "Do you know who killed my brother?" Once you find out, your response is, "Fuck them. Just fuck them. And their whole set." That's when you got a gang situation. All of it is really, really deep, and there aren't any simple solutions.

There are three levels of gang membership: the *hardcore,* the *members,* and the *affiliates.* The *hardcore* gangster is the straight-up warrior. He's always out looking for the enemy; he's always in the attack mode. He lives the violent side of gang life and that's all he focuses on. He's equal to the army soldier who enlisted in order to go to war. "Fuck the GED. I'm here to kill some muthafuckas." He's the guy reading *Soldier of Fortune* magazine and living for the confrontation.

The *members* are in gangs primarily for the camaraderie. They'll represent their set, but they're not the guy who's sitting there nutty, just ready to go at it all the time. The members usually run the gangs because they are more levelheaded than the hardcore member. These are the guys who understand gang membership has its privileges. The Geto Boys have a song out that's titled, "Damn, It Feels Good to Be a Gangster," and the members have fun with it. They gain brotherhood and confidence that they aren't getting from anywhere else.

The *affiliates* know all the gangbangers, and they wear the colors. But they are not out there putting in the drivebys. Usually, they just live on the same street as a set, and they abide by the rules. Sometimes, the affiliate gang members might be calling the shots because they may be a little bit

■ I rap for brothers just like myself,
■ Dazed by the game, in a quest for extreme wealth.

more intelligent and nonviolent than the other members. I was an affiliate member, and if one of my homies from Hoover needed advice, we'd hook up and discuss tactical maneuvers. Before you know it, you're setting up a drive-by.

When you live on a certain street, you will always be held accountable for your 'hood if something goes down. In other words, a totally square kid living on 83rd Street knows his street is a Crip street and knows he can't avoid the politics of his 'hood.

I once went with my daughter to buy some sneakers. I picked out a pair for her, but she pointed to a red pair: "Let's get these." I looked at her and asked, "Red, what are you talkin' about?" But she was living near the jungle off King Boulevard and Dorsey High School and that's a Blood area.

She let me know she's not a gang member, but she's part of that environment. She told me, "I'd just rather blend in than try to fight it." If she wants to wear blue and all her girlfriends are wearing red, she's gonna create a problem, so why do that?

The first three levels of gangs really have to follow the rules completely. One of the main violations is associating with the enemy. It's like the Civil War revisited down in South Central. If you have to visit your cousin on Sunday, expect to hear about it on Monday. "Yo, cuz, I seen you with them Bloods." Kids get sweated for that all the time, because they got gang spies. If you're seen hanging on enemy turf, it's like an act of treason to your set.

The rules of gang warfare are not much different from the U.S. military. If a fight breaks out, and you run, you can get smoked for that. In the army, you could get sentenced to death. So, the kids who are more blatant with their membership—or in military-speak, gung-ho—gain the rank. In many ways, gangs are playing the same games America plays against other countries. It's a game of superiority being played out on a smaller scale. But it's essentially the same game.

The ultimate rush for any man is power. When you're in a set, you not only gain power, you gain rebellious power. You're now not answering to anybody. Once a kid can click this switch in his head and say, "I can do what I want to do. I'm here on this earth and there are laws, but I'm gonna handle it my way," his ego's boosted. He gains identity. Any time you join a fraternity, you immediately become somebody, even if it's only in your set.

In the ghetto, just the names of these gangsters have their own power. If I say I hang with Tony Bogard, everybody in the hood knows who he is. He's the guy who initiated the gang truce, and he's as big a gangster as anyone. Why does Bogard have juice? Because he's been shot a bunch of times, and the kids over there know he's not afraid of anyone. The buzz around town will sound like, "Oh, you know him? You know Raider from Santana block?"

Who are these guys? They are not professional athletes or pop stars. But they are big shots to the ghetto kids, because they got their names from being tough. They didn't have money, so they used the one commodity they did have: strength.

Gang culture is ghetto male love being pushed to its limit. Gang members wear their colors in defiance of everything— in defiance of the cops, in defiance of other sets, even in defiance of the school system. When they wear their colors while strolling through rival turf, it's called bailing, and to anybody on the outside, they're *insane*. Why would you just walk down the street like a big target? Because in an aggressive environment, it's your way of saying, "I'm not afraid of anybody."

■ **One wrong move, and your cap's peeled.**

Gangs offer security to kids in a fucked-up environment. It's not the killing that initially draws a kid into gangs. It's the brother-like bond, because you're telling the kid, "Yo, I love you. And nothing's ever gonna happen to you, because if anything happens to you, those muthafuckas are going to be dead." You don't tell your girlfriend that. You don't tell your mother that.

They follow true on that promise. When you see these drive-bys and kids are hitting five or six people on the street, they are retaliating for the murder of one of their boys. I've seen crying men enter cars and when the doors shut, they go out and murder.

If they hit their target when they put in work, most of them will walk. They know that in Los Angeles if you go out and kill another black man, odds are you aren't going to jail. Your case isn't an LAPD priority. It's the old ghetto saying: "A nigger kills a white man. That's murder one. A white man kills a nigger. That's self-defense. A nigger kills a nigger. That's just another dead nigger."

If your case does make it to court, the witnesses they'll try to use against you to send you to jail are usually from another gang. These kids want to see any member from the other set go to jail. And once your attorney proves this, you're not going to jail. You're not gonna get popped for it. That's what is so ironic about the Rodney King trials. The witnesses for the defense were police, and that should have been a conflict right there. They are in the same gang—*Of course* some of them will lie to save their buddies.

Most of the gang killers are still out there on the street. I meet kids every day who are introduced to me as "the shooter." "This is the shooter. This is our killer." Which means this kid has killed and will kill again. This is not only what he does, it's what he's known for. Sometimes, they won't be much older than fifteen or sixteen years old.

■ I ain't no superhero, I ain't no Marvel comic,

30

When someone tells me, "This is the shooter," it means he got away with it a few times, and he's not afraid to do it again tomorrow. Getting away with it once is all it takes. In his mind, he's saying, "It's on."

Gangs have been able to get away with so much killing it just continues. The capability for violence in these kids is unimaginable. Last year, five of my buddies died. I don't even go to the funerals anymore. It's just so crazy. There are just so many people dying out there. Sometimes, I sit up with my friends and I think, "There will never be another time on earth where we'll all be together again." A lot of my original crew is dead. You get hard after a while. You get hard. People on the outside say, "These kids are so stone-faced; they don't show any remorse or any emotion." It's because they are so conditioned. They are conditioned, like soldiers in war, to deal with death. You just don't know what it's like unless you've been around it.

In L.A., gangbanging is done under the supervision of the police. The cops watch the gang's activity—they don't get in it, but they allow it to go down. They don't care about people hurting each other. They'll allow Al Capone to do his business, but don't hurt them. The gangs are not out to attack the police. No Mafia messes with the police, because they know the cops will come down if you hurt their own.

The gang mentality is, "This is my city, this is my 'hood, this is my world. Fuck the police. They are here to do what they got to do, and I'm here to do what I got to do." They have total disrespect for the law. Don't put them on any different level than any other gangsters—Capone or Bugsy. They had no respect for the law either. They knew the law was there, but it was simply something to get around.

They say, "We've got to go in and do our business and some of us are gonna fall, and some of us will get hit." But

■ But when it comes to game, I'm atomic,

the gang members feel they are surviving, and they aren't really doing anything wrong. They are looking at poverty as being wrong. They figure they ain't got nothing, so fuck it.

Poverty totally instills a "Fuck it" attitude. "What am I gonna lose?" It ain't like they're coming out of nice houses in Brentwood and going out and taking a risk. They are coming out of the projects. Their homes might be as big as the average living room. My buddy Malik will tell you, "Man, I got a wife, four kids, and two pit bulls in a single apartment. So don't come tell me what to do. I'm in here just trying to live. I'm coming out here on the streets and whatever I got to do, I got to do."

Stories fly around town about cops antagonizing gang members to fight each other by going from set to set and spreading rumors about who murdered who. A lot of cops find this shit funny. If you're a real policeman, you don't want to see anybody get hurt. But you got to first put yourself in the mind-set of the cop who gets up in the morning saying, "All these fuckin' niggers, savages down here. I'm gonna go down and put some of them in jail and beat some of them up." That cop, he's causing just as much trouble as they are, because he's in there stirring them up. They'll pull you to the side of the street and tell you to get out and run. They'll tell you to fight them, and you've got to fight them.

The gangs do nothing more than act as defiant as possible toward police. A gang member will see a cop and throw his set up to him by using hand signals. They call that "giving it up" or "hitting 'em up." Like Ice Cube says on his *Predator* album, "See One-Time hit 'em up." He's illustrating the defiance gang members feel toward One-Time—the cops who roll through the neighborhoods. Most gang members aren't afraid of getting thrown in jail, because what do they have to lose? To most of them, jail is no different than home. They ain't gonna do nothing but kick it with the homies in jail.

■ At droppin' it straight, point-blank and untwisted,

32

Everybody's there. You ain't got nothing on the street. So if you get popped, so what? If you're young, you say to yourself, "I can do two standing on my head."

Gang mentality is totally pounded into your head in prison. When you go to a prison in any section of California, you get thrown into a "car." A car is the group you hang with when you're in the joint. A ride. These are the guys you'll be rolling with in a prison riot. The first thing you'll be asked after being in prison for a while is, "What car you in?" In jail, there are Muslim cars; 415 up north; 213 in L.A.; Black Guerrilla Family; a Crip car, a Blood car. These cars are your gang and your form of protection while you're serving time.

Like in any gang situation, even if you don't side with any of them, that becomes a car—the people who ain't with anything. An inmate will ask, "You ain't with the Aryan Nation? You ain't with the Muslims?" If the answer is no, you become linked with all the other prisoners in an independent car.

If a convict goes to prison for ten years and lands in a Crips car, he's waking up every day, putting on his bandana, walking the walk. And it's no joke—when a guy who outranks you in your car comes up to you and tells you that you gotta stick some guy, you gotta do it.

There is lots of drama in jail. By the time you come home, you're really banging. When the police take you off the street and put you in jail, your criminal side is totally reemphasized. You'll see the gang tattoos. You'll see the change in their eyes.

My hope is the gang truce can reach into the prisons because the prisons are what really run the streets. In the joint, you get favors by seeing what you can do for somebody on the outside. If I were in jail with you and you wanted something done by me, or I wanted something done by you,

No imagination needed, 'cause I lived it.
This ain't no fuckin' joke,

33

I'd say, "Don't worry, I can reach your people and handle what you need." So, a lot of the guys who are getting killed on the streets are being reached by people in the joint. The joint contains the most hardcore gangsters.

The prisoner's mind-set is, "I'm already in jail, right? I can handle this for you. Your problem's gone." So all these shots are getting called by people in the joint, and if they decide the war is over in there, then it will be over outside, too. You can't stop on the outside without the commitment of guys in the joint. They're gonna be saying, "Yo, when I get out: Blam." It has to happen in both places simultaneously.

One of my buddies once told me, "Man, everybody wants to be special." If you can't be special by being the smartest person in school, you're gonna try to be special by being really different or really tough. The guys in Boo-Yaa Tribe wear these big braids, and they'll take a little girl's blue barrette and clip it to the end of their hair. Now, they know that looks crazy, but what they're saying is, "I'm gonna look crazy. And if you don't know better, you might say something to me about it." It gives them a distinction.

I went to the Mann's Chinese Theatre in Hollywood one time with fifty of my gangbanging buddies, right? Fifty dudes with sunglasses and baseball hats. You should have seen how the streets cleared as people got out of the way. These are kids who would never have seen that kind of power without being in a gang.

When killing becomes involved, it turns into a real dark, evil thing. If they only threw fists when a confrontation came up, there wouldn't be a problem. But somewhere along the line early on, somebody got killed, and once death came into the equation, it became a very dark, very evil, scary thing.

Whenever somebody gets power, it's inevitable it will get

abused. Gangs are no different than any organization. It's not good enough to be a football team and stroll around and be nice. It's much more fun to wreck up the club.

They do what they gotta do.

In Kenneth M. Stampp's book *The Peculiar Institution*, Frederick Douglass is quoted from over 140 years ago as writing, "Everybody in the South wants the privilege of whipping somebody else." He believed that slaves, by having to submit to the power of their masters, therefore became aggressive toward each other and would whip each other even more cruelly than their masters. Frustration builds into aggressive behavior and it causes people to lash out and hurt somebody else. Anybody who suffers some kind of pain is searching to reach out. If you grow up in an aggressive environment, your threshold for pain grows higher and you're gonna do one of two things: You're gonna become extremely gentle or you're gonna become extremely violent.

I'm more or less a gentle person, but I have the ability to get extremely violent under stressful situations. I'm the person who's pleading. "Let me be nice, okay? Will you please let me be nice? I want to be nice."

Because I have a gangbanging past, people always want to test me. That's a dangerous thing, trying to push the ghetto button. People could end up dead in these situations. With gangs, you are dealing with killers, or with people who have the potential to kill. Why would you want to fuck with this guy? Why would you want to try to see if he's real? Because of his upbringing, the ghetto black man has this mechanism built in him he's trying to control. Voyeurs shouldn't push him toward the edge. Sometimes, you're dealing with people who are so frustrated, they are almost on the brink of insanity. They even got a Crip gang called the Insanes, probably because of this.

■ **Two weeks ago, I was out at the disco.**

The way to deal with these guys, especially when they're attempting to break out of the gangster mind-set, isn't by threatening them. In Orange County, California, politicians are threatening to crack down hard on gangs. They actually believe if they bully these kids, they will be scared out of gang membership. "Yeah, we'll scare Johnny, and he won't want to be in gangs anymore."

They don't have a clue that by the time a kid joins a gang, he's already lost all fear of what could happen to him. Nothing could be scarier than Johnny's home life and his upbringing. The killing fields have destroyed his spirit and the lives of his friends. If they were smart, they would be exploring the issues that make a kid want to join up in the first place. Why does this kid want to tag on the wall? It's so typical for the government to say, "Let's go after the kid instead of figuring out the reason he's so full of hate. Let's attack Ice T because he wrote 'Cop Killer.' We don't want to explore the reason he might have written it. That's too horrible. That's too complicated."

Because the causes are never explored, the battles will probably continue. With the injection of drugs into the gang world, you have the perfect breeding ground for organized crime.

People outside of the gang arena will always have a difficult time understanding why these kids sell drugs. They ask, "How could they hurt their own people? Why would they do that? They are hurting themselves." To understand this whole thing, I always use this scenario: Take four people, put them in a prison cell, and say to one of them, "Come to work for me. First off, none of y'all are ever getting out. You're destined to die in this prison cell. But if you poison the other three, I'll let you out. They are gonna die anyway. But you can be the one who lives. I'll allow you to kill them."

■ Two brothers stepped up to me and said,

How many people in the world would be able to stay there for a hundred years and die with these people or just take a chance to get out? That's what these kids are saying. "I ain't got no way out. It's not that I want to hurt anybody, but this is my chance. I really believe the chance of escaping outweighs the harm I'm doing to other people."

When you deal dope, people are coming to you and begging you for it. You don't really see you're hurting anyone. You're quick to say:

"If I didn't give it to 'em, somebody else would."

"They want the dope. They want it. I'm fulfilling a need."

"They're feeling good."

"Well, it's their own fault, you know."

"I got to do this. For the first time, my little sister got new sneakers. My mama's car note is paid. I'm able to achieve something. I'm having things now. I ain't never had anything."

As a dealer, you become intoxicated with what it gives you, and you can't stop. People don't go into selling drugs to hurt people. If that were the case, they would take the drugs and lace them with cyanide. They are not trying to kill anyone, they are trying to get into an occupation that allows them a chance to live better than they are. Before the introduction of crack, you had units of kids that were out there fighting each other over a street, not money. Now, all of a sudden you gave them a chance to make a cash flow and these kids created their own organizations.

Dealing also helped break the gangs up into smaller units because they had the money and the opportunity to do it. Right now, crack cocaine is the number-one employer of minorities in America. It's very hard to retire from that occupation.

That's capitalism right there. Crack and cash flow has

"Hey yo, Ice, we don't think you're down,

given yet another angle to the whole complex problems of gangs. Now you see the gangs spread out all over the United States, and you wonder where they come from.

They took the game on the road. The crack or dope you sell here is four times as expensive out of the state. Los Angeles right now is the number-one headquarters for cocaine in the United States. It's no longer Miami. This is the dope capital. They stopped coming in through the Miami borders, and now they're bringing it up through Mexico and Arizona, and the drugs hit in L.A. first. The gangbangers will get it, and they're already organized. Everybody's got a cousin in St. Louis or Cleveland, and they can fly out there and get their homies involved in the drug trade.

A gang member will fly out to see his relative, and since he's already got an identity to the relative, the kid out of state will listen to what he has to say. Gangsters are given respect because compared to these kids in Missouri, they've got it going on. A kid in Mississippi has never seen anything like it. He's dirt-ass poor, saying, "Hey, I wanna be in this. I like this."

The L.A. connection will tell him, "I'm from the Rollin' 60s, and I've got this product for you. If you have any problems or any drama out here, I'll have muthafuckas flown in from L.A. You see how we're kickin' up dust in Los Angeles?" And in no time, they'll turn out about ten dudes in Mississippi. They'll dress 'em up, teach them the ropes. And now Mississippi's got a gang, with real members.

Then, just like organized crime, they decide they want to take over an area out there, and they need somebody to handle it. So they fly in another kid from L.A.; he does the job and he's out of there. Straight hit. And how are you gonna bust this kid? This kid's not from Mississippi. Nobody knows anything. Nobody's ever seen him. He doesn't even know anything about who he's doing. And it's on.

■ **What set ya claimin'?" 'E drew the Glock, yo my set's aimin'!**

38

The gangs grew out of control in L.A., so they were able to spread throughout the rest of the country. The problem's gotten very complex and very deep. We're looking at the breeding grounds for a black Mafia. The irony is that it's always been this way. A lot of the immigrants who came to America applied their own criminal tactics to try to get ahead.

With the onset of the gang truce, the gangs in Los Angeles are in their final bonding stages. Prior to the truce, the gangs had all bonded into small units, which I see as a death bond. If they remain separate, the war would definitely continue. By bonding together, they can step back and realize, "Yo, we've all got the same enemy. Let's stop killing each other." You would have a devastatingly, not only powerful but dangerous unit of black men in Los Angeles.

This is a situation the LAPD does not want to see happen. They do not dig this gang truce. They want to keep them separate. Once you sit down with twenty thousand guys who used to be fighting each other in groups of five or five hundred, and you set them all together, you've got some kind of new phenomena. Think about the force of these kids for a moment. If you ask, "How many people here have done a drive-by?" and two thousand hands go up, you've got some shit on your hands. You've got some hardcore soldiers. And if they decide the cops are the enemy, then the LAPD is in trouble. The cops have every reason to want these kids to remain separate; it's better for them if the kids keep killing each other.

I'm not even worried about the gangs all banding together. Once they really reevaluate their lives, they'll want to move in more mellow directions. When I was out there hustling and looking at everybody crazy, I believed that was what I always would have to do. Once I was able to change and once I had hope for a different future, I didn't have those

■ **Dumb muthafucka try to roll me, please!**
■ **I'm protected by a thousand emcees**

feelings any longer. I didn't really want to hurt anybody anymore. I had no pressing reason to go out and do low. But when you're down in that hole, you feel like that's how you've got to be all day, everyday.

The whole gang attitude is something you have to be brought slowly out of. Lots of brothers can't do it. The deejay I work with, Aladdin, grew up in Compton, and even after we started working together, he used to go back to Compton every night and hang out with his homies. I used to tell him, "Yo, Aladdin, you look like a gangbanger." It was cool he was going out there to hang with his buddies, but I knew that if they committed a crime or hurt somebody, Aladdin would be nailed because he was making records. The cops could get with him. You have to remember, the brothers he's rolling with have the ability to disappear, they're unknown. That's why gang members have nicknames. The worst thing you can do is call a gangbanger by his last name. They purposely keep themselves incognito.

Aladdin knew what was going on, but he'd tell me, "I come over here and kick it with you and it's cool, but I got to go back to Compton, man. When I go back to Compton, just because I know you, everybody thinks I'm a little bit better. So I might have to stand out on the corner with my boys for an hour or so—and I might not even want to—just to prove I'm still down."

I told him he's got to start protecting himself. They might try to make him do low just out of jealousy, because they know he's got a chance to get out. His true homie will be happy for him, but these other guys might challenge him by daring him to out and commit a crime with them. They might try to test his loyalty. That's when Aladdin needed to step off and tell them he's not really down with that. He'd found his way out, and he was getting paid. If they can't understand that, then fuck 'em.

■ And hoodlums and hustlers and bangers with Jheri curls;

40

Eventually he had to get an apartment and move out. But he didn't just move, he took his real friends with him. They still come over and hang out. 'Cause even when you're in the neighborhood, you might seem like you got a lot of friends, but you really only got a couple of really true friends.

I never see the elimination of gangs. I would like to see the elimination of gang violence, though. Currently, I'm putting a lot of time and energy into Hands Across Watts, the organization in L.A. trying to see the gang truce through. Many of my friends still live in South Central or Compton, and every other phone call I get is word from the street. I'm what you call a shot caller, so I probably know more about what's going on in the 'hood than the people who live there. I'm paying for funerals and counseling kids to quit killing over colors and streets. I'm their homeboy who made it, and I'm trying to set an example that there are alternatives to violence. I have hope that peace can be instituted.

If you could just get the violence down to a standstill, you'd be left with what the rest of the world calls clubs. In a city this big, you need a group of people around you. When I was in the army, whenever we left the post the sergeants used to tell us to go in a group. "Take a gang," is what they were really saying.

The United States Army is one big gang. The cops are a gang. When they come, they come in units. So the theory of telling the kids to walk alone is bullshit. When you're in an angry environment, you need a friend. I tell women all the time to take a girlfriend if they're going out for the night. Walking alone ain't healthy when there are people out there to prey on you.

Now if you're a girl, you might just go out with your girlfriend—two might be enough. But in a rougher part of the city, you might be better off to go in threes or fours.

■ **We won't even count the girls.**

41

When you're from a rough environment like South Central, you need to ask yourself, "Are we going out looking for trouble? Or are we going out to protect each other?" The organization I created, the Rhyme Syndicate, is a business. But at the same time, it employs ex-gang members and ex-street hoods and in a way, we are a gang because people know they don't want to fuck with us. We're not looking for trouble, but we got each other's back if anyone tries to fuck with us. They are my insurance. This is nothing new. The Mafia uses the same tactics. Any organization—the FBI, the CIA—is a club and if you fuck with one member, they'll call for backup.

People have got to understand that gang warfare is not something that should be treated like some minor problem. It's gonna take a big truce. It's gonna take negotiations, and it's gonna take money. It will require a lot of effort to get it to end.

Thousands of people have died on each side of this bloody battlefield, and it's not just something that you can snap your fingers and tell people to stop. When you talk to these kids, they are like veterans from war. If you went to Beirut and asked a kid about his life, he wouldn't tell you he's at war. He'd just say, "This is how it is. You know, bombs and shit going off. I grew up with this, so this is how it is."

They are used to death. They are used to despair.

On my song "Colors," I rapped:

> **My color's death**
> **Though we all want peace**
> **But this war won't end**
> **Till all wars cease.**

■ **'Cause they got my back and I got theirs, too.**
■ **Fight for the streets, when I'm Oprah or Donahue.**

42

This gang war is just like any other war. If you think it can be easily stopped, let's go to Northern Ireland and tell them to stop. Let's go to Bosnia and tell them to quit. Don't call it anything less than what it really is. Now, once we accept that, we can begin to deal with it. As long as the media define the fighters as dumb gang members, they are undermining and not really seeing what these kids are going through.

We can say how stupid it is. We can say how ignorant it is, and I'll agree. But understand that you can say that about any war. Regard it as such.

Whenever the U.S. goes to war, there is a reason for it and there is money for it. But in reality, I can see more sense sometimes in this war out here in these streets than in some of the wars people are shipped overseas to from America. They are usually fighting something they don't even understand. They are fighting for a belief system that is American, when these kids are out fighting for somebody who hurt their family. They're on some real shit. Until you've been up and around 250-pound dudes crying while loading guns, you don't know what it's about. You don't know this is real. Why did it happen? I don't know. But the problem, the reality, is somebody's dead, and somebody wants revenge.

But that's just my opinion on the killing fields, who gives a fuck.

■ They try to sweat a nigger, but they just didn't figure,
■ That my wit's as quick as a hair trigger.

3
Crime and
Punishment

Everybody in the world at some time or another commits a crime. Everybody is a criminal. The first time you drive one mile over the speed limit, you've committed a crime. The first time you don't come to a complete stop at an intersection, you've committed a crime. The person who cheats on his taxes—even a little bit— is committing a crime. The question is, how far will you push the limits of crime? How far are you willing to risk getting busted? Do you do it for a profit? Here's the bottom line: Does crime become your occupation?

It's so easy to understand the temptation and lure of crime. You've seen all the money the DEA pulls off drug raids. Anybody who has looked at that for one minute and thought, "Damn, if I just had one of those stacks . . ." has fallen under the influ-

Crime is an equal-opportunity employer.

■ "He's not your everyday-type prankster."

44

ence of what makes people commit crimes. For that one moment, you took a step toward it.

Now, take that one step further by adding a guy who whispers in your ear, "You want it? I can show you how to make it." In the streets, that guy is in your face all day. I've watched gangsters dump $400,000 onto a bed in a motel room. One-hundred-dollar bills took up the entire bed. This wasn't a movie starring Demi Moore and Robert Redford, this was the real shit. I looked at that cash and thought, "Damn, these are just some brothers." They weren't no CEOs from Warner Brothers. They weren't no big executives. These were just my homeboys.

At the time, I had just gotten out of a four-year stint in the army. I'd joined the military to do the right thing after getting a girl pregnant in the twelfth grade. I was in some hardcore infantry shit that preached the "Kill 'em all" approach, just pure gung-ho shit. I hated the military, and when I got out, I just wanted to be a deejay. Like everybody else in the army, I came out with a whole bunch of stupid-ass stereo equipment. Equalizers, turntables. I ended up working a government job, and at the end of the month, I got a check for $180 every week. After taxes. Fuck, my homeboys were driving Mercedes Benzes. So I started rolling with them. I became Ice T on the streets before I was Ice T the rapper. I had a name, a Porsche, all this shit, but all I ever really wanted to do in life besides be a deejay was be a pimp. That was my real goal. I'd even named myself after a pimp, Iceberg Slim. But to be a good pimp, you have to be your own best ho. And pimpin' wasn't really about enough money. So my crew and I turned to hustling. Not hustling in the white sense of the word, but ghetto hustling—insurance scams, burglary, jewelry heists, armed robbery, whatever. Once the money starts coming in, you're hooked.

I'm Ice T, the original gangster.

45

■ ■ ■

Anybody outside of the crime world has to ask themselves a few questions: Do you believe people commit crime just out of hate? Do you think people break the law out of necessity, out of poverty? Or do you think they just want to break the law?

There is a small group of people who break the law out of straight-up anger, who are mentally unstable and just want to hurt people. There are even a few rich people who like to commit crimes for some thrill, just to get a rush. But most people commit crimes because they didn't think there was any other way for them to get over. They didn't think they had a chance. When I was heavily involved in crime, I didn't think anything was wrong with what I was doing. I didn't think I was doing anything to hurt anybody else. There are all kinds of different criminals. Believe it or not, criminals have rules and moral codes. Some criminals don't give a fuck about anything, others won't commit an act against a person, per se. They'll focus only on businesses.

When my crime crew started out burglarizing, we were on that level. We didn't want to deal with people. We didn't even want to come in contact with people, which is different from a robber. A robber will walk up to a person, but a burglar just wants the merchandise or the money in the safe. We aimed at businesses, which we perceived as part of the system. The truth was the companies usually had a lot of insurance and would claim they lost more than they did anyway. So, everybody's out screwing everybody.

We used to feel like we were doing them a favor. If we robbed a jewelry store for $100,000 worth of goods and they claimed a $150,000 loss, how many months would it have taken for them to sell $150,000 worth of jewelry? It might have taken them six to eight months to sell it. So, in one quick move, they move up a year in sales. It was to their advantage, and this wasn't lost on them. As you get deeper in, you would find people who would set up their own burglaries. "Okay," the owner would say, "I'll leave the door open. Here's the combination to the safe. Later." Ooh, it got really deep and complicated.

When I was hustling, I never clouded my mind with drugs. Drugs make people scandalous. When you combine drugs with crime, you have a criminal who just doesn't give a fuck. A guy who might not have hurt a person sober will now use force. Users need that dough. Your survival becomes intertwined with your dependency. If drugs were legalized in the same way alcohol is, fewer crimes would be committed right off the top because so many crimes are directly related to illegal drugs. I don't believe anybody will ever be able to control any substance. Anything that a chemist can make will always be available, period. You'll never be able to control alcohol. You'll never be able to control heroin. You'll never be able to control crack. If crack were available right now through the American government, all the money they are using for drug enforcement could be used to create total awareness about what drugs will do to you. Through ads and education, the government could raise user awareness. The money could also be spent on rehab, so addicts wouldn't have to get on six-month waiting lists when they decide to clean up their act.

So much violence follows drug use because users are always scrambling to get it. Everybody's using dirty needles, and the government just watches it happen. There has to be a reason our government does not legalize drugs. Somewhere somebody must be making money, because I just don't believe they care that much about people. How can they be concerned about drugs when alcohol abuse has the same effect on the body as crack?

■ Got on your bulletproof? Well, mine's goin' right through.

There should be harsh penalties, however, for drug-using parents or for mothers who indulge in drugs while pregnant. The same penalties should apply to alcohol intake. As far as I'm concerned, drugs may as well be legal because you can *get* them. People who want to shoot heroin, shoot heroin. At this moment, the problem is the violence that follows illicit sales—cops raiding people and people shooting each other.

Now that alcohol is legal, you don't see people murdering each other over whisky anymore. That war is gone. People need to understand that any substance available on earth will be obtained by the people and used by the people. All you can do is accept that fact and make life safer for everybody involved.

Crime is like any other job. The more intelligent criminals get involved with more intelligent forms of crime. And the more ignorant people are stuck on the lower rungs, like muggings and stickups. "Give us your money" is about as simple as a crime comes. Burglars might have to use a tool or know how to disarm an alarm. They need to have some smarts.

These guys will probably move up to fraud—paid arson, insurance fraud, credit-card fraud, which are all rampant at this point. A popular insurance scam in L.A. is the crack game, or the forced accident. These guys are looking to get hit by new cars, which are generally insured. The person in the crack-game car will attempt to hit the driver as he makes an illegal turn or doesn't come to a full stop.

Even though they hit you, you were in the wrong so you can get sued. In this game, the attorneys are crooked, the doctors are crooked—everybody knows what's going on. You can walk into a crack-game attorney's office one day as Joe Schmo and the next day you can tell him your name's Ronald Reagan. They don't give a fuck. They are making a lot of money. All of this drives up insurance premiums for people, but what does the criminal care? He doesn't have insurance. He's just getting paid. Who is the bigger crook here? The hustler or the "respectable" lawyer or doctor? Without them, there's no game.

As you get deeper and deeper into crime and you watch your cash flow build, you eventually learn you're going to have to kill somebody. That's the dangerous part. Full-fledged career criminals have to play hardball. They can't view anything as off-limits or illegal.

You enter a warp where you say, "If I got to kidnap somebody, I got to kidnap them. If I got to kill them, I kill them." You can't at any point say, "I won't do that." That's the only way you can survive full-out with the criminal life and really make it big. If you start selling ten-dollar bags of weed, that might get you a nice car. But if you want to get a real nice car, you have to start selling pounds. You want to get a house, you're gonna have to start selling ten, twenty pounds of weed. Once you hit this level, people know you. You've made yourself bigger, and you've become more of a target for the lowest form of criminal: the robber. The robbers are just waiting around for someone else's bags to fill up. So you might have to kill them to protect what you got. You're more likely to be victimized by a robber than a legit person is. Robbers know they can rob a drug dealer, and the dealer ain't going to the police. So they'll come and victimize you.

You also become intoxicated with the game of it all. The smart drug dealer isn't getting high off his dope, he's getting high off his cash flow. You not only employ a lot of people now, but you're accountable for a lot of people's money.

Say there's a kid in South Central selling dope. If he's got a connection with the Colombians, he can't quit. The

■ Without respect from the streets,

punk kids on the street who help sell can't have you quit, because the next man might not use them. The Colombians can't have you quit, because you're moving too much dope for them. They'll put you in a coffin. You can't quit. So you can get yourself in a jam where you just can't stop. Now that you're hustling, you've got a lot of overhead. You've got a house you owe on, you've got cars and bills. Before you got in the game, you could've lived on nothing. But now, you need fifteen Gs a month just to keep the shit you got. No hustler ever wants to sell his shit. You get caught out there. Nobody wants to start moving backwards. To a hustler, that's more stressful than coming up. That's why you see very rich people do very crazy things when they think they're gonna go broke. You see them kill somebody in their family for the insurance money. They go to extremely scandalous and drastic measures not to go broke. I'm much more afraid of somebody who's rich and on the verge of going broke than of somebody who's broke and trying to hustle a meal.

But a criminal has to ask himself, "Do I want to kill somebody? Do I really want to go that far?" Because eventually you'll have to go that far. Either somebody won't keep his word, and you'll have to step to them. Or word will get out on the street that you were screwed and the dude didn't have to pay. One way or another, in crime you end up having to get violent.

That's what turned me off to crime. I never had it in me to go out and hurt anybody. I was the kind of criminal who wanted everybody to play by the rules. "Damn, why can't I just do this and you pay me and everything's straight?" In other words, I was looking for honesty in crime. But the key to understanding crime is that everybody's a criminal. Everybody you deal with is a liar and a cheater and a sneak and a double-crosser. So it's a very strange world, and it makes you very aware.

■ So I don't claim to be the hardest muthafucka on earth.

50

■ ■ ■

Crime is more addicting than any drug. Beating the system is the ultimate rush. You learn that as a kid. Stealing a cookie out of the cookie jar is a thrill. You scored. There is just something about getting away with it. Whenever you can outsmart the person in charge, that's the shit.

Ask yourself, "Who's smarter? The cops or the crooks?" It's got to be the crooks. A cop's job is to watch this line between right and wrong. And if anybody steps over that line, they're supposed to catch them. So he stands there and stares at the line. The criminal's job is to figure a way to step over the line and step back without getting caught. So he has to think about how to make this cop look the other way. When he scores, the adrenaline rush kicks in and he's off planning the next crime. In the film *Point Break,* they combined the ideas of surfing and robbing. They explored the total rush these guys were after.

The adrenaline rush is just so dope, it can't be compared to anything else. Once you become successful, you're addicted. If you're good, it's extremely hard to stop, because crime's an excellent-paying job.

My crew excelled at jewelry heists. We started with picking locks—"trimming"—then moved over to "bashing," smashing the outside glass of the jewelry stores and taking the jewelry. That's why I got all these big cuts on my hands. We weren't pistol bashing, we would show up unarmed. This way, we were less likely to be shot at. When pistol bashing became more common, we moved over to "snatch and run." We'd walk into a jewelry store, ask to see expensive pieces, and just start running. We wouldn't pick just any store. We'd already cased a store that didn't have guns. We'd park our car two blocks over and walk the escape route backwards. We wouldn't just run out not knowing where we were going. We'd hop a fence, shoot through an apartment building with

◗ Catch me slippin', I can even get worked.

doors already jammed open in advance. Even if the store owner had a gun hidden away, we were out of the store so fast—I mean, we were moving.

These days you might have to go to Nebraska to find a mall jewelry store with no armed security guards, but that's what you'll do. You'll find a slow town, fly in on a hot credit card, rent two cars, get a return ticket. Hit the store, jam out the front door, switch cars, drive to the airport, and leave the car running. You're out of there.

You've just committed a federal crime. The F.B.I. can go after you, but the cops can't chase you because you've broken federal lines. And who are you? Where did you come from? Nobody knows. By the time our crew disbanded, we were international. When one of my boys got busted, he had fifty-two aliases and warrants in twenty states.

I was lucky because I knew when to say no and that kept me out of a lot of trouble. I just knew when to say no. Fortunately, the statute of limitations has gone by on all the crimes I committed. I'm also fortunate I never killed anybody, not that I know of. Sometimes, a lot of bullets would fly but it would be a damn big surprise to me if a bullet I shot hit somebody. It would wake me up and scare the shit out of me. Let's hope not. That's another book.

Despite all my material possessions, I'd committed crimes for a number of years and hadn't gotten extremely rich. I bought my share of toys, and my crew was well-known on the underground in L.A. But all of a sudden I started watching a lot of my boys going to jail, and I knew I was ready to slow down and slack off. I hadn't gotten that much out of it and now the boys I could really work with were gone. All these secondhand players were just running around. I looked at our crew and I thought, "Who really got rich?" None of us.

■ But I don't slip that often. There's a coffl

We were able to sustain a fly lifestyle, real flash and all that, but there wasn't that much money.

When I stopped, I had about $80,000 in cash and assets. The reason I totally stopped was the film *Breakin'*. My boys told me, "Yo, you should do this, man. You got a chance." So I did it, and I immediately went broke. I ran through the cash without even feeling it. I was still living at that speed, and I had to go through withdrawal. I really had to stop myself. Every other minute I thought, "Damn, I could go do a lick." My friends stopped me. They were still hustling, and they would come over and offer me money just to stay down. They wanted to see me make it out. One of my buddies told me, "Ice, man, you need to do this movie, man. White people like you. You got a chance, man."

In a way, it was a really sad statement because he was saying, "I can't make it over there. They won't let me in."

Crime is an equal-opportunity employer. It never discriminates. Anybody can enter the field. You don't need a college education. You don't need a G.E.D. You don't have to be any special color. You don't need white people to like you. You're self-employed. As a result, criminals are very independent people. They don't like to take orders. That's why they get into this business. There are no applications to fill out, no special dress codes. In crime, you only need one thing: heart.

If you talk to girls who are into crime, they'll tell you, "Hey, I get up when I want. I do what I want, I like that." There's a degree of freedom in being a criminal. But you're always gambling with your freedom.

You have to ask yourself how much you are willing to risk your freedom. Before you get into the game, you've got to know how you'll adapt to jail. How much risk will you

■ **Waitin' for the brother who comes up soft when**

take, and where will you draw the line when it comes to jail? Now, some people can do time. Some people can *do* time. I, for one, *cannot* do time. I do not like doing time.

If you don't have anything you'll miss on the outside, or anyone who'll miss you, then doing time won't be such a big thing. You'll adapt. If you're living in a little bullshit place, you won't miss it.

In jail, they are taking away your freedom and your contact with females. They know the male sex drive is very important, and taking that away, man, that really creates a lot of madness down in there. Some guys will masturbate, some will rape other convicts. A lot of guys who aren't gay will find themselves having sex with men. And still others will decide mentally to learn to maintain and overcome it. It is definitely an extremely stressful environment.

I have been incarcerated on a lot of occasions, but I've been very lucky. I've never been what's known as "stretched." Stretched is where I would get served with a prison term that's a year and a half or more. I've looked at two-year to five-year stretches. I've looked at a lot of different prison terms that never got to court—either I wasn't convicted or I wasn't held long enough to see the trial.

When you're hustling, you learn there are lots of ways you can get out of court. People use aliases or get bailed out and never return. You've got to have cash and you can only do it for so long. There are all kinds of ways you can work the criminal system, but I can't give that much away. I fear giving up too much of the game. The last thing I want to do is write a how-to book for criminals. My homies will read it and say, "He told everything. What the fuck are you doing, man?" They say the game is to be sold, not told. Besides, half the fun of beating the penal system is discovering your own tricks.

When I think of all my buddies who've done stretches,

I feel so fortunate. I fiercely did not want to do time. And my mind was never muddled by dope, so that worked in my favor. I know I was just damn lucky. All my friends went to prison. One of my buddies is getting transferred to Marietta Penitentiary in Illinois. He went in initially for seven years, but he could have been out in three. Right now, he's on eight and a half.

People have no idea that you can get served a year and end up doing life. Within the jail, you never know what could happen. I could go in there for a week and some guy could try to take my manhood. He's either gonna rape me or kill me. If I kill him protecting myself, I get a murder rap. So now my little one-week traffic-warrant slipup has turned into murder, and I'm in there for life.

You do one of two things in jail: You either decide you're never coming back, and some light goes on in your mind, or you find yourself back on the street committing another crime. You don't know how many people I talk to on the phone who tell me, "I got something, man. Ice, I'm gonna come out and in twenty-four hours I'll have a million dollars." They've been in jail five years plotting it.

You can never recover that time. That's the biggest mistake. Robbers sit in their cells thinking, "I wonder who's on the streets making my money for me?" In his mind, some kid's out there hustling his turf and as soon as he gets out, he's gonna aim a gun in the kid's direction and say, "Thank you for making all this money for me. I'm back."

The prison system is a very dark world, and believe me, it's not the answer. The government seems to think the answer to crime is more prisons. Let's just build more and more prisons and let's incarcerate more and more people. For some unknown reason, with crime, just as with gangs, they refuse

■ Take a look around,
■ All them pussies can be found,

to go into the reasons for the problem. Around twenty years ago, the government decided that criminals can't be rehabilitated, so they went into this mode of crime and punishment. They feel they can punish you to your senses.

On my album *Original Gangster*, I say: "Slavery's been abolished except for the convicted felon." So, indirectly, I think their answer is just to create these big cages and put everybody in jail and hold them tight. Taxpayers don't know this approach costs more than leaving people out on the street and giving them a chance.

I would never have gotten into crime if I'd had a decent education that geared me toward a job. If I came right out of school and had even the slightest hope I could get a decent job, I would've taken it. Now, I truly believe the prison system is big business and that it seems to be more important than education in this country.

The government is currently building a prison in Lancaster, California. On the news they announced that it was gonna bring in millions of dollars in revenue each year. The penal system is one of the biggest corporations in America right now. Incarcerating people is big money. The more criminals, the more money.

Handling problems that lead to criminal behavior doesn't profit anyone but the future criminal. That is what lies at the root of the situation. If I was born Ice Huxtable, and my father was a doctor, I might have a chance. I might have a chance to go to school, and I might see the benefits of being a doctor. The only reason I would ever get into crime would be out of curiosity or laziness, not out of necessity. Why would one of the kids on *The Cosby Show* go out and commit a crime? It's not even in their attitude. Most of the kids who go out and commit crimes are coming from broken homes where there's no real cash flow.

As long as you believe certain people are always gonna

■ **They talk a mean fight but fight like hos,**

be criminals, the only solution the government will offer is building more jails. "Let's just get these people off the street and put them where you can't look at them."

Each one of us has a criminal in storage we pay for and we take care of through taxes. It's as if they are put into this attic in your house you never go to so you can avoid looking them in the eye. I'd rather take my money and send my criminal to college, give him a chance to get a job, so he can be a productive part of the system. Most people don't even know that it's cheaper to send your criminal to college—even to a private college—than to keep him in prison. At Stanford, you pay around $21,000 a year to send a person to college—but to keep your criminal in prison, you're paying $47,000 to $75,000 a year!

If you decide to send your criminal to Berkeley or UCLA, you can probably foot your neighbors' bills and send nearly a dozen criminals to college. America would be the most heroic place on earth if we were willing to take a real look at these kinds of options.

The hardest task for a criminal is taking that first step toward the other side. Once you're on the street and you've gained criminal knowledge or criminal notoriety, you gain respect from your peers in the underworld. But in straight society, that respect won't transfer into the workplace.

Now all of a sudden, someone's telling a guy—a big-shot hustler who was on the street making money—to go empty those fries. It takes a very strong person to be able to deal with that kind of change. Whether you approve or not, this guy used to have the prestige of running his own business. He had status. So it's extremely hard for him to make the transition.

That's why I'm out there looking after them, and if they come work for me, I'll give them that respect. I'll tell a guy,

"I know you're a bank robber. I respect you. I know what you are, man. And you ain't no punk, so we're gonna work together on this." I deal with them very carefully. I know how difficult it is for them to be told what to do, but I explain that they are here to work. It takes about six months to a year to ease them in.

I still go through that with my organization, because I hire expert con men and thieves and liars. Luckily, I'm better than them. I know what's going on, and before it gets deep, I'll approach them and say, "Don't try that. That ain't cool. . . ." And we'll work it out. But in a regular work environment, they are not gonna get that kind of treatment. They are gonna have a real problem fitting back into the system. Most of them were never a part of the system to begin with.

When a convict comes out of prison and ends up in the workplace on the bottom of the scale, you're saying to him, "You should be happy, you were just in prison." He views prison as having pressed a pause button on his life, and he'll maybe do that menial job for a little while, but don't try to tell him he should be happy.

People commit crimes because they need to boost their self-esteem. In the crime world, you can gain self-esteem without waiting for the system's approval. Even gang members are kings in their world. So handle them correctly. Whenever I shoot one of my videos, I'll bring some of my gangbanging friends and inevitably I watch them snap. The directors and the production assistants are running around giving orders and pushing people around—this is especially amusing when we're shooting in the 'hood—and by the end of the day, my guys are saying, "Fuck you. Fuck your video. This is my neighborhood and you're a guest here, remember?" This shit is real.

Having connections with people who do not give a fuck

■ **Snatch you out your car so fast you'll get whiplash**

is a very important association in business. Businessmen are aware that the criminal's mentality is one step over the line of standard business practices. When I bring my friends with me to a meeting, I'm subconsciously saying, "We can do business, and if you are totally honest, there will be no problems. But I know people who could give a fuck about your fucking contract, a fuck about this record label or this movie company. I know people who will burn this muthafucka down. You would never find a social security number or any trace. I got the loose cannon, the wild card, the joker called the streets on my side."

The Mafia uses the same tactic. If you meet somebody Italian, they'll never tell you they ain't got contact with the Mafia. They'll always say, "Well, you know . . ." They like to leave that little gray area, because that's the area they can use to assure them you won't fuck them out of a contract.

The scariest element in America right now isn't even the Mafia. I think the government's scared of the kids on the streets and of the person who has access to that type of power. It's not like the kids on the street are holding any weak cards. They are holding big cards, and they deal with big business. The government knows that.

There's definitely something sexy about crime. It takes a lot of courage to fuck the system. That's why women like an outlaw—because this man is going against the grain. Anybody can go along with the move; it's so simple to conform.

I've sat in a room with women and said, "Right now every cop in America hates my guts. You're sitting in a room with one of America's most wanted and hated criminal activists. They are probably looking for me right now." They get off on that shit, like they're in the room with John Dillinger. Depending on your perspective, going up against the man, the government, and risking your life out here is the

■ Numbers on your rooftop, for when the copters pass.

ultimate turn-on. It takes courage. People are quick to call criminals cowards, but crime takes courage. No matter how bent or wrong it is, you're taking a risk. Too many people live their lives without taking any risk at all. The same kind of girl who will be attracted to criminals will also like a guy who surfs or sky-dives, because it's all dangerous.

The biggest criminals in this country aren't the street hustlers or the men behind bars. It's the people who are behind the actual control of the drug trade. Drugs are supposedly illegal, but somebody is allowing the drugs into the country and somebody is calling the shots. They are probably part of that small, nameless group of men who actually run this country.

Maybe it's just several different police organizations who are willing to take payoffs, but the floodgates are open. If that's the case, until you legalize drugs, more crime prevention has to occur within the ranks of the crime-prevention organizations than among the people on the street.

The second-biggest criminals are the oil companies—all the big corporations that deal in pollution. These are the companies that portray themselves as all-American while they're out there fucking up the air and preventing technology from advancing in order to fill their own pockets. They fight all the environmental organizations, and they win because they have more money. They are as terrible as any drug dealer because they're pushing a toxic environment on you. They are arch-criminals. But you'd be hard-pressed to send any of these executives to prisons for their crimes against humanity. They are waving the flag while paying everybody off. They'll never see the inside of a prison cell.

It's so strange to have friends in prison. It's like they're dead, but they're alive. You just don't see them or hear from them much. If they are in the hole, you can only talk to them once

■ Gangbangers don't carry no switchblades,
■ Every kid's got a Tec 9 or a hand grenade.

a month. The hole is the equivalent of solitary confinement, and you just get crazy. It makes you crazy.

The whole jail system is there in order to make you crazy. My friends in jail are the reason I'm not there. Guys who went in when they were eighteen and are coming out when they are thirty miss a lot of their fucking lives. My job as a friend is to tell them, "Don't rush it. Don't rush it, man. Move back into this slowly."

The only people they know are crooks, because legit people don't deal with you while you're in prison. You don't even know how to talk to them. You're so distanced from what's going on now, and you're bitter because people will tell you you're dated. You become even more alienated because you can't even tell some people you were in jail. The penal system is such a vicious cycle. You come out with no money. If you write "convict" on a job application, you simply ain't getting hired. So you're stuck. How are you gonna come up with a first and last month's deposit on an apartment? To get the money you need just to climb back onto the other side, you're almost forced to commit another crime. And crime is the only job that will employ you without discriminating.

Your only hope is to run into some buddy who made it to the other side. It's like Jim Morrison's lyric "Break on through to the other side," except these guys aren't trippin', they are just trying to get to the side that the privileged are born into. If they can just find a small opening, they're in. If you run into that person who will respect you, you're in. You got your chance. But if you don't run into that person, you find yourself back with your crime buddies. You don't have to explain yourself to them. You get sucked back in. People are so shocked when they hear a convict committed a crime right after getting out of prison. But what were his options? Once they get you in that cycle of prison, it's hard to get out.

■ **Thirty-seven killed last week in a crack war,**
■ **Hostages tied up and shot in a liquor store.**

You've also got a tail on you, which is your parole. Legally, you're still owned by the prison. You're just doing time on the street. If you get caught around anything illicit— even if you're not involved—you're back in.

Three of the guys who work in the Porsche shop I own are on parole. They're living in a halfway house set up by their parole officers, and they have to be in at night. You might be there for a month and that's how they slowly let you out.

I'm very proud I associate with convicts. In actuality, America is starting to build a convict and an ex-convict culture. Soon, everybody on the street will have been in prison or will be connected with somebody in prison. At the rate the government is locking people up, over the next fifteen years, 20 percent of the people on the street will be ex-cons. In 1991, 42 percent of Washington, D.C.'s, black males between eighteen and thirty-five were either in prison, on probation, or out on parole.

What this means is, the next time you meet somebody behind a desk, they may have a relative locked up, and they might be sympathetic toward hiring you. They might give you a chance to get over to the other side because they might understand where you've been. This convict subculture will be very powerful once it gets established.

The cops have made a point of saying they don't give a fuck about me, because a lot of my friends are convicted felons. Being black and going to jail is almost like a rite of passage. You're gonna go. You're fucking lucky if you're from the ghetto and you never went to jail, because they work on you so hard. My buddy, Sean E Sean, a/k/a Little Sean, was busted selling weed in high school. Everybody knows somebody who sold weed in high school, but how many of them got a year in prison?

He came out after a year, and in no time, he was stopped

■ **Nobody gives a fuck. "The children have to go to school."**

62

by the police on his way back to South Central. He had a gun in his truck. Why did he have a gun? Because he lives in South Central Los Angeles, and he had a gun for protection. He wasn't jacking anybody. He went back in for a year because he was caught with a gun while he was on parole.

The biggest crime he committed was selling weed, but now he's done two years. When he gets back out, his truck is parked on the side of his girl's house. The cops are raiding a crack house next door. He walks outside, and he sees the cops rifling through his truck, and he says, "What the fuck are y'all doing? What are you doing in my truck?" They decide to search his girlfriend's house, and they find her pistol, registered to her. He's still on parole. He didn't even know she had a gun, but he isn't supposed to be in this house with a gun while on parole. He's thrown in prison for another year.

When I went to San Quentin and rapped for the prisoners, some of them told me, "Ice, man, you're the the one who got away," and they were happy for me. The fact that brothers in prison respect me is more important than getting respect from anybody else. These guys have made their mistakes, and they are doing their time, but they represent the real heart of hardcore street America. This is where you end up. So I need to continually ask them, "Am I doing the job? Am I telling them how it is?"

"Yeah, you're telling them, man."

A lot of the guys in prison don't like rappers who seem to glorify crime. They respect the way I deal with it. I talk about it, but I let you know it's real. In "Original Gangster," I said:

**I'm a hardcore player from the streets,
rappin' 'bout hardcore topics,**

■ **Well, Moms, good luck.**

63

over hardcore drum beats.
A little different than the average, though;
jet you through the fast lane,
drop ya on death row.
'Cause anybody who's been there knows
that life ain't so lovely on
the blood-soaked fast track.
That invincible shit don't work.
Throw ya in the joint,
you'll be comin' out feet first.

All of the rappers who act so hard and act like they ain't gonna get caught, if they got thrown in jail, they'd die. This invincible shit is just not how it is. I'll show you how funny it is to wind up in jail. I'm not gonna go out there and tell kids—or anybody who's listening—that this is something you can get away with forever.

If they started throwing privileged people into the general prison population, they'd have to change the prisons. If you're only arresting underprivileged people, how loudly can they complain about the prison conditions? Who's there to listen? Put one rich kid in there, all of a sudden his father's calling the governor and making some changes.

Most of America is so oblivious to prison. They view criminals and prison in the abstract. When I rap about these issues, I think it really affects the conservative factions in this country. They don't want you to know how it really is. The fact that you don't know where I've been is one of the reasons everybody's so ignorant. You can't judge a man until you've walked in his shoes.

How many people do you know in jail? How many people do you know in a gang? How many of your relatives have died by gunshot wounds? How many of your friends

■ **'Cause the shit's fucked up bad, I use my pen and pad,**

died in the last year? How many people do you know personally who are homeless?

If the answer to all of the above is "None," you're not even qualified to comment on these issues. You have to decide how real your life is in comparison to what I'm talking about. If you're getting information from the news, then you are seriously misinformed. Fuck the news. None of the anchors have ever been in jail. The newscasters are out there patronizing the fuck out of every ghetto person they deal with.

For all the negativity surrounding prison, you can use the time to your own advantage. On the outside, you're too busy hustling to stay alive to take time to analyze yourself. In the joint, all you got is time. You can flip it around and use the time to gain knowledge and gain strength. You finally have an opportunity to get what you should've gotten up front: an education. If you can load your head with the right ammunition, you won't go back. If your head is still empty, or if your head still has a big question mark in it, you will end up back in the penitentiary.

In California's Pelican Bay Penitentiary, they've started taking away your library privileges. You can't even send a convict books; the warden sends them back. Think about what they're doing. They are taking away your chance to enlighten yourself. They've already taken away your contact with people—no visitors, no letters, no books, no TV. They break you down to nothing.

All you have contact with is more inmates. If you lock a dog in a closet for a week, he comes out crazy. You lock a man in the hole for six months, you can forget about him. My buddy was in the hole on and off for about six months, just total blackout, living in a room no bigger than a bathroom. In Pelican Bay, the yard is as big as a bed. You're standing there, you're outside, you breathe the air, then you

■ **And my lyrics break out mad.**
■ **I try to write about fun and the good times.**

go back in. Everybody up there is on max. You're not allowed around other people. My buddy is on lockdown twenty-three hours a day. He stays in his little cell twenty-three hours a day. He's been doing this for years. When you turn a person like this back loose on society, he's gonna need somebody there to really let him in, somebody with money. You got people hitting these streets cold turkey, and it's so rough. And the police will taunt you and say, "Bring your ass back here. We'll keep you in here."

If this is the way the government plans to continue running the penal system, they might as well just continue to build prisons. It's inevitable the prison population will continue to increase and increase and increase because nobody's dealing with the root of the criminal behavior.

Law enforcement isn't really trying to stop crime. Crime creates so much money for the economy. When we go to war, it stimulates the economy. So does crime. There's more money made on the cleanup of drugs than on the selling of drugs. If you sell fear, you'll sell car alarms, home alarm systems, bars on windows, guns, steering-wheel clubs. Who's out advertising these anticrime devices? The cops. If you eliminate crime in certain areas, you lay off police officers. A nice undertone of crime keeps everybody employed.

Even if you're deeply involved in gangs or crime, if you're smart, your crew will deter you from crime. If you were gonna go hit a bank, and one guy on the crew is a good basketball player, you'd ask him, "Why you ain't playing basketball, man? This is what we do, but why aren't you shooting hoops?" Or if the guy was a computer nut, his crime crew would tell him, "Yo, you need to be at home working on your computer, partner." That's what my guys did for me. The fucked thing is, everybody should be able to do something other than go out and commit crimes. They shouldn't have

■ **But the pen yanks away and explodes**
■ **And destroys the rhyme**

66

to be put in a position where it's inevitable they're gonna grab you. Once you're caught, there's nothing saying you'll ever return from that lane.

If I went to jail tomorrow, they'd put the squeeze on me. My record has gang activity, right? So they wouldn't put me in with the general population. They'd put me with the gang-bangers. I'd have to immediately braid my hair back up, and I'd have to be off in there with the locs. In the past, the inmates in my set might have wanted me to kill someone; but now, in my position, I'd have to be a shot caller. I'm the one deciding who's gonna do what and who's gonna kill whom. All of a sudden, I'm back sagging, and I have to readapt to that environment in order to do my time. That ain't no way to live. It's total, total madness, but this is how it is.

That's just my opinion on crime, who gives a fuck.

■ Maybe it's just 'cause of where I'm from. ■ L.A.
■ That was a shotgun! ■ O.G. ■ Original gangster.

Part II

A PIMP'S GUIDE TO SEX, RAP, AND GOD

4
Men, Women, and Sex

I can't speak for women, but I know what men are about. I know about muthafuckin' men: They want to fuck. Men are dogs. They would like to sniff it and fuck it, *now* if not sooner. Men reading this right now are shaking their heads and saying to themselves, "Damn, Ice, shut the fuck up."

As kids we are taught to make you believe we have other reasons to talk to you. At school, we'll walk up to you and ask, "What's your name? How are you doing?" But what we're really saying is, "Man, I want to fuck you." This is what drives the male. Women should give me a special service award for tipping them off.

This instinct is simply *in* men. That's why a little boy will open up a *Playboy* magazine and get an erection. He's never seen a naked woman,

Life is X rated; it's not rated R.

he does not know what his dick is for, but he will have an erection because the feeling is innate.

Women do not want to believe this, but sex is the only thing men are thinking about when they initially step to you. When you walk into a club and you go after a girl, you don't go after her because she's a monster in your eyes. You go after her because she's attractive to you sexually. After you get to know each other, love may take over and the relationship becomes something deeper, but the first level is always animal attraction.

The male sex drive is so powerful that if it were to be eliminated, the entire economy would crash in one day. There would be nobody at work, nobody in school. All we would do is lie around and eat and fart and get fat. The sex drive is what makes men get up in the morning. It's the machine that runs the world. Why do men want to become successful? To get women. For gay men, it's no different. You're ambitious to please your partner. If women didn't like criminals, there would be no crime. If a thief knew women wouldn't accept the things he buys with stolen money, he wouldn't steal. The money would be no good. Very few men are out there seeking just straight-up blatant power. In the film *Scarface*, Al Pacino says, "In this country, first you get the money, then you get the power, then you get the women." He didn't say, "First you get the women." Women were the prize at the end of the climb.

The sex drive is so powerful that a man literally goes into this warp where he will do anything for his woman. This is called *hard dick insanity*. I've been on that insane chemical before when my girlfriend was coming to meet me in New York. She flipped my switch and started talking crazy to me on the phone. Next thing you know I'm out at the jewelry store getting her presents. I lost my mind, because passion causes you to lose your mind. Passion makes the world go 'round. Love just makes it a safer place.

For those of you entering the partnership race, I've devised a Relationship Meter to help you detect compatibility. In every relationship, there are four different areas you need to be totally aware of:

> Physical attraction
> Mental attraction
> Mental compatibility
> Physical compatibility

PHYSICAL ATTRACTION. Guy looks at girl; girl looks at guy; guy looks like Godzilla: Ain't shit happening. You're fucked. If the girl looks like Roseanne, you say, "Ehhh, I'm not turned on." You have to have some sexual attraction for this to rise to the next level. With sexual attraction, you're saying to yourself, "I don't know when. I don't know how long, but I can imagine myself with this person intimately." If you look at a guy and cannot imagine yourself with him intimately under any circumstances, you're only going to end up friends. "Friend" means, "We won't fuck, friend. You're my friend, you're my brother." You ain't fuckin'.

MENTAL ATTRACTION. Physical attraction can be enhanced sometimes by mental attraction. You might find a business associate so mentally attractive you start seeing a physical attraction. But you didn't come in looking for it. You got hooked because you're working an intense job with this guy, and even though you found him ugly, his mental attractiveness starts intriguing you. You may look at him and say, "He doesn't really look that bad. His stomach ain't that flabby." In a club, that would never happen, because you're

■ As far as Pops, I don't give a fuck what you do . . .

out looking for people who are physically attractive to you and the mental attraction comes later.

MENTAL COMPATIBILITY. If the first thing that comes out of an attractive man's mouth is, "Let's go shoot some heroin," you're out of there. He may look nice, but he's a chump. If he says something interesting, and the girl is receptive, you probably have the beginnings of mental compatibility. You'll exchange telephone numbers maybe, but you're not going to have a one-night stand. Mental compatibility is usually determined pretty early on.

PHYSICAL COMPATIBILITY. You touch. You kiss. You hold. You'll either hit or miss.

If you hit on all four of these, you'll have some form of a relationship. Whether it's an affair or boyfriend-girlfriend-type relationship will be determined by how high you're hitting in each category. If you have high physical attraction and high physical compatibility, you might end up just being fuck partners. Now let's say those two factors don't fit: You think, "I don't dig him physically, and he can't kiss, but we learn from each other when we're together and it's fun." This is a strong, nonsexual friendship.

Take three out of four. He's good in bed, he's nice-looking, he's okay to be with, but at times he's annoying. He can't be a total thing, but you don't mind going out on a date with him. If somebody hits on all points, you're in a real dangerous situation because you could fall in love.

This meter is extremely important. When your girlfriends ask you, "Why are you with him? He treats you like shit. He doesn't ever come around. Why do you constantly go to him?" You know it's because he's hitting on one and four. They don't understand, because he's hitting the *fuck* out of four. You say, "You won't know, baby, because you're not there, but he's hitting the *fuck* out of my four."

Or maybe *she's* hitting the fuck out of four. Pussy-

■ Bust him in his muthafuckin' head.
■ If he got any money, take it.

whipped: "I can't control it, man. I can't control it. Shit, that girl calls, I come."

"She's wrong for you, she's fucking you up."

"Fuck it, man, I can't help it—she's got me."

With that scale you can always find out where you're going. The hardest thing is to be honest and grade truthfully. You can look at your partner and say, "Well, he's attractive. Well, shit, he isn't really that attractive." This is the hardest thing in the world.

Because love is conditional, the scales on the meter start changing. People start skipping. Maybe the guy's getting fat, and passion needs to be regained. Most of the time, the relationship deteriorates because people start getting lazy. It's not like you're still working at it like you were. You're not going out together anymore, you're not dressing up.

When you first went out, you'd look sexy for each other. You knew how to turn each other on. You can rekindle a romance; it's not that hard. I'm still excited in my relationship, but you got to work at it. I'm lucky because absence does make the heart grow fonder. Sometimes I think we've been together so long because I'm away a lot.

People generally have to make an effort. The classic scenario: The guy says, "Damn, baby, you ain't putting on that lingerie anymore. Why you wearing those granny dresses? What happened to my little sex kitten?" while he's sitting around with his belly hanging out. Or worse, the squirrel mentality sets in. You've found the nut, now you're gonna bury it. You don't want your woman to look sexy anymore because you don't want her to attract other men. This same guy will take his girl out and cover her up, while looking at other women. This is an insecure guy, and that's a male problem.

The most difficult thing for a man or a woman to deal with in a relationship is watching it slip away. When that

■ **If there is money in there,**
■ **Rob the motherfucking joint.**

happens, you have to admit it's going, and it's not coming back. It takes strength to fall in love, but it takes real strength to walk out when it isn't right. I had a girlfriend who I spent a lot of money and time with. I attempted to mold her the way I wanted her to be. You can't mold anybody. They're gonna be who they are. They can only fake being the way you want them to be.

I went through this whole trauma. I didn't want to be embarrassed by losing her. My ego was saying, "Leave all the shit that was mine behind." I was trying to repossess the things I had given her, but really deep down inside I was saying, "I don't want you to go. I just want you to change." When I realized she wasn't going to change, I also realized she was a pure bitch for a lot of other reasons.

To walk out of a relationship is hard. Nobody wants to believe they spent time believing in something that wasn't real.

Real relationships require compromise. Love is not a selfish game. At times, you will have to rub his neck. Maybe you are dead tired, but he would really like it, and you love him, so you rub his neck. There are gonna be times when she's gonna want something, and you're gonna have to accommodate her. These usually aren't requests that money can buy. These are physical acts of unselfishness over selfishness. This is what real love is all about.

In any relationship, you got to know who you're going into business with right up front. I'm on the road a hundred, two hundred days of the year, and there is no way I can get around the fact that I meet women all the time. That doesn't mean I'm going to necessarily be with them, but I enjoy their company. I can't pretend something may not happen either. But I don't give my girlfriend any reason to sweat me.

The day a girl pops up at the front door with a suitcase,

■ **As far as Moms, bust her in her goddamn head.**

my girl and I will have a discussion. Either that, or there will be a girl at the front door getting her ass kicked. By the same token, I'm not going to interrogate her when I get back into town. I'm not going to take her through this nightmare inquisition, "Where were you? Who were you with? What were you wearing?"

Our philosophy is realistic. When I'm here, I'm here. When I'm not here, I'm not here. When I come back from a tour, she'll ask me how the tour was, and that's it. I'll ask her how Mexico was if she spent the time traveling, and we move forward. What's happened has already happened, and there's *nothing* we can do about it.

Some things are better left unsaid. Anybody who tells you they would rather you be totally honest is lying. Your girlfriend might say, "Tell me, tell me, tell me. At least be honest. I want to know." She's really saying, "Lie better than you've ever lied in your life."

People who do have open relationships should remember three key things, because there are gray areas that can cause nuclear explosions: Don't even think about practicing anything but safe sex. Stay away from all friends and relatives. And finally, if you are to have an affair, always sleep with somebody who is at least as attractive as the person you're with. If you're caught with a monster, a fat girl, or someone she feels is less than her, she'll be totally ripped apart because her ego will be hurt.

The worst retaliation is to sleep with one of your boyfriend's friends. His buddy. One of his guys who comes over to watch TV with you. You are really trying to end up dead over some shit like that.

All women, in the deep, dark recesses of their minds, know men fool around. Whether they have sex or not, a lot of men need to periodically have their ego catered to and that occurs only by conquest. A woman will walk out of the house

Dumb bitch, that's the reason we're going up in there—

and men will whistle and let her know she looks good. But men don't get this treatment.

Most men could go a year without anybody saying, "You look good." So how does he determine whether he still has it or not? He has to go out and try to talk to a woman. If the girl smiles, he's still got it. Reassurance may be all he needed.

A woman must know man's nature: It is a woman's nature to covet. It is a man's nature to conquer. Point blank.

For women, there is one guy out there—I don't know if it's Michael Jordan or Tom Cruise or Arnold Schwarzenegger—but there's one guy in your mind, and you'd fuck him if he gave you the chance. There would be no conversation, there would be no dinner, there would be nothing but straight fucking.

Girls will ask me, "How do you deal with these girls who just want to come to your hotel room and fuck you?" I reply, "Well, I don't know. I might be this guy. This guy who they have pictures of on their walls. They watch the videos. They've waited and all of a sudden I'm there. They're on a mission."

I won't be inviting them all in. I'm not crazy. In show business, you're not just the average guy a girl meets out of nowhere at a restaurant. She's had time to watch you. Listen to you. Read articles on you. Read your book. Watch you on TV. Rewind you on video. She's probably slept with you in her mind fifteen or twenty times already. So when she meets you in the flesh, she's gonna go for it. Whether you're Jon Bon Jovi or Axl Rose, if you fulfill her fantasy, she's completed this mission.

The average guy has to find out if he's even close to her vision of the ideal man. Then he's got to determine how long it will take for her to be with him. This requires straight

■ **She don't know what the fuck she's talking about**

78

military tactics. So, apply the Relationship Meter and determine where you fit it. Qualify the customer. Are they even buying today? If the answer is "No. No. No . . ." then why are you even going to try to talk to this person?

There are various lines to keep in mind. "You probably wouldn't go out with someone like me, right?" Here, you're attempting a little reverse psychology. Most girls aren't even tacky enough to say, "No, I wouldn't." They'll say, "Why would you say that? 'Course I would." But if she adds the critical follow-up, "If I didn't have a boyfriend," you're out of there.

One big problem with a lot of men is they think they can talk to every woman. Because once, on a good day, a super-attractive woman might have stepped to him. So he's thinking that the girl across the club should fall for him because she's less attractive.

No. No. No. To some women, you'll be attractive. To other women, you will not be attractive. It does not matter who you are. You might be the flyest model in GQ, and to one girl you're gonna be The Shit, and to another you will be monster.

Once you establish that, you can get into the game. The line works for both men and women. If you don't want to play any games, you can just say, "I think you look good. I don't know you. But I'd like to talk to you. Am I bothering you? Let me know? I'm not trying to have a one-night stand." They'll answer yes or no, but get to that first. Don't spend the whole night buying drinks. Don't be afraid to see if you're in the ballpark or not.

Once you get in, it's your turn to show them how great a person you are. It's time to be funny, it's time to be deep. Whatever direction this person wants to go, you gotta be able to blow in it. Hopefully, you are already somebody this person likes, because you can't really be anything you're not.

◀ Everyone get back, this is a rap jack!
◀ I'm taking your kids' brains, you ain't getting 'em back!

If you are only out to fuck, do not be afraid to lie. Do not be afraid to *lie*. Do not be afraid to say whatever the fuck she wants to hear. "You've got the tiniest waist I've ever seen." Tell her whatever she wants to hear. Lie. Lie. Lie. Lie the fuck out of it. You are just trying to fuck, you're not trying to be her man. She's probably trying to fuck you, too. Maybe another way. Maybe she's trying to get drinks out of you.

My buddy Bango, in Cleveland, had an answering machine by his bathroom that had a special tape I made for him. As soon as a woman would step inside to use the bathroom, he'd hit the message playback. First three girls would call, "Bango, where are you?" "Bango, what's up?" "Bango, call me." Then my voice would come on and say, "Bango, what's up? When are you gonna come out to L.A.? I've got the check for $150,000 you're waiting on. Also, I need you to find some girls for us to shoot 'cause we're gonna work on this film. Check this—you're gonna bug out, man, but Eddie Murphy saw you in my video and he wants you in his film. He wants to talk to you. So, you've got to be ready to fly out. Okay?" I would sign off and then there'd be one last phone call from another woman.

He told me as long as he lived in that apartment, which was only a year and a half, a girl never came out of that bathroom till that machine stopped playing. He'd fuck every night off that tape. That tape got him crazy pussy. If a girl is willing to fuck you because of a tape like that, then she deserves what she gets.

During this process, a game is going to be played on both sides. If, at the end of this lying procedure you turn out to like each other, you can back out of your lies by saying, "You know what? I was really just trying to get with you. But you're really cool. . . ." She might leave, but if she's real, she'll understand.

■ **With a move of perfection, my dissection;**

When I met my girl, I just walked up to her and said, "Do you wanna be on an album cover?" I didn't have a record deal. How am I gonna get her on an album cover? But I sized up the situation. She was out there dancing and probably wanted to be seen, so I came up with this line, "Do you really want to be seen?"

As you get older, you don't take the same approach. You go from "I want to fuck a girl" to "I like the way she looks, I wouldn't mind being able to know her over a period of time. I don't know how deep it will go, but this is somebody I might not mind having *down* with me." The urgency is gone. You can be real.

Younger guys got to hustle. I know guys who have ten different business cards for whatever floats a woman's boat. These are operators, and they are good. And there are women out there who are just as good with their drag. They'll play you off like they're from Beverly Hills when they're living in a single apartment and are completely broke. They've got a broken TV antenna with foil sticking off their set. They'll have all the gear, and they'll look like models, but when you really get to where they are, they're broke. It's the same hustle. It works both ways.

Whenever a girl who can't make ends meet puts on a Chanel bag and hits the street, "Yo, I'm popping," she is full of shit. A girl isn't gonna walk up to you and say, "Yo, I'm broke," and a guy isn't either. Unless they're real.

If you're clever or charming, you'll always find somebody who thinks you're interesting. This, however, is the problem. A lot of guys aren't clever or charming. They ain't got no flavor about themselves. They're just blah. That's their problem, and they got to work on that. I can't tell them how to be charming.

My whole point is you've got to have some kind of plan that factors in two equations: First, you have to meet some-

■ **Some call it a lethal injection.**

81

body who doesn't think you're ugly or you stink. Second, you have to be half-assed clever, you have to be somebody worth meeting. This won't work for some bum lazy muthafucka, because he's just fucked. You got to make the effort to make yourself into something.

Men have to learn courting and mating skills. You can help yourself by learning a few basics. If you can dance, that will help. Give a woman a reason to like you. Wash your ass. Do some sit-ups. And once you get your physical act together, read some books. Learn something. Be interesting. Get some flavor about yourself. Most important, get in the game.

Once you've established you're in the game and you've made a date, here are the key lines that will get you sex. Use what I call the power of suggestion. The power of suggestion is the biggest weapon anybody has in their arsenal. "There's no sense in me and you worrying about sex. Because if we hang around each other long enough, it's inevitable. I don't know if it'll be five years, but we will eventually have a close encounter."

You're going for a yes answer, because you're saying you are gonna fuck sooner or later. You got to know when to say that, when to hit it. What you're saying is, "I'm not going to rush you. I'm not tripping. 'Cause I can just tell off the vibe we got that if we were to hang around, shit would hit the fan. And when it did, you'd need the fuckin' exorcist here in case somebody floated over the bed; you'd need to take the smoke detector's batteries out, and they'd have to keep monitoring the Richter scale at UCLA 'cause this shit will be raw. There's no sense in even tripping, 'cause it'll happen one day."

This girl will laugh, she'll smile and think, "Goddamn, this muthafucka's bold," but deep in her head, if she does imagine it, one day she'll have to agree with you.

■ I'm gonna fill 'em with hard drums, big drums,

82

Now, you have to turn the clock up. You have to make five years become tonight. So you then take an approach like this: "Who says what's right? What's the time limit on passion outweighing love? Why are all these boundaries in your head? Probably because you've run into some bad experiences.

"Do you know what you want? Can you reach out and get what you want? Or are you gonna wait for what you want and play games?"

Now, if you think she likes you, you tell her, "This is what I find attractive. A woman who sees what she wants and moves on it." You're turning the clock up as you go. You're saying, "Be bold, be reckless. Move on it."

Confidence is the greatest aphrodisiac. Overconfidence is a turnoff. It must be handled like nitro. My girl is very extroverted. She's always been that way. If I had to beg her to dress sexy, I wouldn't get off. The most erotic thing to me is to hook up with a female who knows what she wants.

The key to my eroticism is submission. Both people have to submit. Now one person's submission might be to dominate the other person. But total submission is the ultimate turn-on. Check out Madonna's "Erotica" video. She's saying, "Yo, I'm going any way you want to go—this way, that way. I'm, like, down with it." *That* to me is erotic. Sexual slavery is the ultimate.

In his autobiography, Iceberg Slim wrote, "A pimp has to have a raw sense of sexuality that will put a nun's morality to the test over long exposure." A pimp has mastered the art of sex because not only can he have sex, he has women who will have sex for him. A pimp's mastery of dialogue is unsurpassed by any lover. A guy can say, "I'm Don Juan, I can lay a lot of women," but a pimp will say, "Yeah, but can you get them to fuck your buddy?"

You have to be able to make a girl want to fuck you

Bitches, hos, and death. Come on and get some

83

without actually moving on her. If you sat up around a nun long enough, she'd probably want to fuck you. And that's the key. That's a whole 'nother warp. You got to deal with them on a mental level, you go to deal with them on a spiritual level.

The average male deals with women on level one. "How you living? Where do you work? What do you do? I have a job, too. I like what you do." But the next level is the key: "Don't you think everything happens for a reason? Don't you feel a vibe? Don't you think sometimes you feel like you're above the rest?"

I'm an Aquarius and while others might think about earth, we think about the sky. I dream. I wanna be with someone who can feel on a spiritual level. This is the spirituality of love. What you're trying to do is form some attachment to this girl that is not of this earth. Like a vibe.

If you can mack a girl out on this level, there is no man who can rival you. You will never be outtalked. You're taking a woman to this level that says, "I don't care if you got a man, I don't care if you got a husband. I don't care if you're married three years from now and got five kids. You and I will always be on this level up here regular people can't understand. We will always be in love."

This can be real. This is not just something you conjure up. In reality, this is how you have to reach all women. It could be conjured and just planted in the brain of a victim. But most of the time, when you do have a good relationship with a man, it is on that spiritual level.

The guy who has that ultimate rap will be able to reach different levels of consciousness with females and the females will understand that. They'll be connecting with him on a whole different plane than the average guy.

I always tell girls I meet when they talk to me they got to be real careful because I'm real good at this shit. I tell them to listen to half of what I say to them, because first of all, they have to understand who I am. If you ask, "What is the fastest country in the world?" it would be the United States, as far as crime and hustling go. If you broke it down from there and took the two fastest cities in the U.S., they would be New York and L.A. L.A. has a more jet-set speed to it, which is based on the motion-picture industry, flashy cars, gangs, violence. New York is a more walk-the-street type of city; a lot more dirt-asshole hustlers, pickpockets.

L.A. is a jet-set-fast city. So we'll give L.A. a faster lane than New York. If you took a pin and stuck it through the map of Los Angeles' center you'd probably come down through the house I grew up in, through the roof.

If you think of what L.A. is and you think what a rapper is, a rapper is a slick talker. Not only does he talk slick, he talks slick in rhyme. We get paid to talk slick. If I'm one of the biggest slick talkers in L.A., and L.A. is the fastest city in the United States, and the United States is the fastest country in the world, you're probably hanging out with one of the fastest, slickest-talking muthafuckas on earth. So the average girl is really in trouble. Be afraid.

In general, the typical person has a two-channel brain: Yes, no. Right, wrong. The objective of a pimp is to open this up to, "Why not? Says who?" He wants to give you cable. "How come? Try this." You've been watching regular TV and all of a sudden you've got cable.

If I can open those channels up wide enough, everything you've ever been taught will be reevaluated as you start using these new trains of thought. You'll do things you've never done, like fucking in a bathroom of a club. You've never done it because you never opened your mind before. It wasn't even in your realm of possibilities.

I'm like a vampire. I can only bring you cable if you

■ 'Cause I got my own opening-dome kit

want it installed. In other words, I can't come into your home unless you invite me in. A vampire is always outside the window trying to get in. Dracula is standing around dressed. He's the plumber. He's everywhere. I'm using every technique I can, but women have to indirectly or directly let me in. They can turn the channel on the TV, and I'm right there going, "Hey, heh, heh," but until they listen for just a minute, I don't have them. People who don't want cable can keep me out by saying, "I know who the vampire is, and I'm not gonna ever listen to him. I *know* I'm never gonna listen to him." But if you crack your door open, I'll get in and your life will never be the same.

I tell 'em, "You better run, little girl, 'cause your boyfriend won't be the same anymore. You'll trip on your parents. It'll fuck your life up." One out of twenty run, but they always come back. You've seen the vampire movies.

Since the beginning of my career, I have been accused of sexism because I am honest and vocal about the way men perceive women. The accusers' perception of me is so far from the truth. I believe the only reason we're on this planet is for men and women to trip off each other. In my work, I deal in sexuality, not sexism. I am sexual. I deal with sex in its most blatant and raw form—real. I've talked to more feminists on this topic than most feminists have, because I travel around the country and deal with them regularly.

If women want to be treated equally, earn equal wages, and attain equal status in the workplace, then I'm a feminist. A sexist views women just as pieces of meat. The fact is, men look at women's butts and women look at men's butts. Is that sexist? At times, people will make fun and treat each other like sexual objects, but do they really feel that way in their hearts?

I don't believe the conflict with feminists is between fem-

■ **And once again I'm gonna put them under my fucking spell**

inists and men. I think the real controversy is between feminists and other feminists. All women want their rights and respect, and that should be dealt with. There are plenty of people who feel this is a man's world, and therefore, men have an advantage over females. I agree that's wrong.

A lot of feminists have very different expectations. They have no consistent definition of feminism. Do women want to get into a foxhole? Do they want to go to war? Does a woman want her door opened for her? Does a woman want to be treated like a woman? Is that a sexist statement? If you want equality, are you looking to lose those niceties? The real war is between the feminists themselves, between the woman who wants to wear a miniskirt and the woman who finds that demeaning.

A woman will say, "My sexuality is something I have, and I don't mind using it to my advantage. I enjoy it. I enjoy wearing makeup and looking nice. This is who I am." If I were a woman, I would enjoy what a woman is. I would enjoy being treated as a woman, and I don't know if I'd want to give up my femininity. Equal rights and being treated as feminine should be two totally different things.

A real live conflict exists with women who can't deal with blatant sexuality. My girlfriend and I went through all this drama when she wore her bathing suit on the cover of the *Power* album. I explained to her in advance what message the image of the album cover was supposed to get across. We were going to show the power of sex, the power of weapons, and the power of deception. I told her to be on the cover she'd need to wear something sexy, and she came out with her bathing suit. She's proud of her body. She had been in a gym night and day, and this was a chance for her to show herself off.

When it hit, men went crazy. Everybody bought the album like it was the greatest thing in the world. A lot of

■ They might start giving you fucking hell,

87

women liked the cover too, because the gun she was holding gave her strength. She wasn't just standing up there by herself, she had a weapon and she looked strong. I've been to more health clubs and gyms, and women come up to me and say, "Ice, I've got her picture on my refrigerator. That to me is *it*." You see, they liked it.

The first thing the critics asked was, "Why did you go out and get a model? That's so tacky. Why would you get a model to try to make yourself look good? She's not in your group. What does she have to do with your music?"

"That's my girlfriend," I told them. "That's my wife." This is how I got married in the public eye. I've never been married—I've never even been to a wedding—but by using the term "wife," that meant I was married.

After this was explained, feminists came up to me and asked, "Why did you make her do that? Why did you exploit her?" It wasn't exploitation. She knew what she was doing. She was down with it. All artists or models exploit themselves. I know I can rap, so when I get onstage, I show it. I scream, I roll on my back, I fall down, I pull my pants down. Whatever it takes. And I get paid for it. Now, if I feel comfortable with what I'm doing, there's no exploitation.

If a girl makes a living getting paid to do bikini contests, somebody will tell her she's allowing herself to be exploited. But she may point out she's making $1,000 a night, and she likes the attention. She just might dig it.

If, on the other hand, somebody is forced or tricked into doing something they do not want to do, then that is exploitation. When you accuse somebody of being exploited, you better ask them first if they were taken advantage of, because maybe, just maybe, they dig it.

Within the core group of feminists, there is little or no acceptance of women who like to flaunt what they got. The truth is, most hardcore feminists I've seen are ugly, and that's

■ **Start changing the way they walk, they talk, they act—**

just the bottom line. They can get as angry as they want, but most of them have leaned toward the more masculine side of life. They want to wear the pants.

Feminists who enjoy dressing sexy are on a whole different level. They just want to get their respect, and in that sense, I think everyone should be a feminist. There's a point, though, where certain feminists begin infringing on other women's rights. They'll look at Madonna and accuse Madonna of denigrating women. That's the equivalent of me saying I don't like gay people because gay men are making men look bad, and if I say that, you'll call me homophobic.

As a straight male, I can say I don't completely understand homosexuality because a man cannot turn me on sexually. I don't know where they get that feeling. It's just like I can't expect somebody from a rich white neighborhood to understand gang membership. It's something so distant and foreign to them. Don't even ask them to reach for it—and don't condemn it, either.

If you took that album cover with my girlfriend on it, and polled a hundred men, and asked them if they preferred her in a bathing suit or coveralls, fifty men would say the bathing suit and forty-eight men would *lie* and say the coveralls, in an attempt to be sensitive. Those guys are probably just trying to fake out the reporter so they can get to her.

There will be maybe two men who really don't want to see her in a bathing suit because they are picturing *me* in a bathing suit. Well, that too is still a sexual response.

A lot of people try to suppress the sexual channel in their brain, but rappers get off on exposing it. They talk about it in a blunt form—with just words and bass, no melody. In music, that's as close as you're going to get to reading a sexy novel. And people get off on it.

2 Live Crew made a living off sex, because people like

■ **Now, whose fucking fault is that?**
■ **The home invader**

sex. They like hearing about it. It's entertainment. There is no limit to the way you can talk about it. Every issue of *Playboy* could show the same girls year-round in different poses, and it wouldn't matter. People would still buy it. Sex is something we are instinctively attracted to. The best 2 Live Crew record ever made was "We Want Some Pussy." When you're on the dance floor, and you're moving in a sexual way and Luke's yelling, "Hey, we want some pussy," what he's really doing is describing the moment. Dancing is like mating. Why not have music that goes along with what you're actually doing?

It takes more than a record to make people want to fuck. If there were a record you could put on that was guaranteed to make people have sex, then I don't think there would be another record ever made. That would be *the* record.

Every guy thinks he has it in his collection. "This is it. This is the record. I play this record, and bam." But I'll tell you one thing, it isn't a rap record. It's one of those Sade records. Rap isn't found in any one of those collections. I think rappers are far from being considered aphrodisiacs. You might put on the rap record after you fuck. But you don't put it on before. Sade is as close as I can come to musical sex.

The people who are most offended by blatant sexuality are the Christian right. They have a certain moral standard that defines right and wrong. To be honest, they have a total hang-up with sex from the ground up.

They feel they should only have it after marriage. They feel it should only be done in the missionary position, and they don't believe in oral sex. I think they're just missing out on the whole reason we're here and what human beings are about. How can they look at an animal enjoying sex and then

■ "Yo, Moms you can basically just suck my dick"
■ This is a home invasion.

turn around and say, "Well we shouldn't do it like that, because we're evolved."

Other religions have a totally different angle on sex. If you read the *Kama Sutra,* they teach you how to fuck down the house. If you try to keep up with that book, you'll be with your girl the rest of your life.

In the past, I've said, "Tipper Gore ain't getting no dick." What I'm really saying is that the Christian right just doesn't know how to enjoy sex. They make rules for everyone else based on their own belief system. Everybody has some form of porn in their closet, but the fundamentalists and the Catholics like to keep it tucked away where nobody can see it. They don't want to see anybody publicly having fun.

The Christian right is quick to call anything they don't want to see in public "pornographic." Life is pornographic. There is violence in the streets, there is violence on the news. To me, that's more pornographic than anything sexual. The injustices and suffering that go on in the streets are pornographic. Life is X rated; it's not rated R.

If a five-year-old child is looking at a porn movie, what is he or she seeing? They are seeing sex, and there is nothing wrong with sex. There is nothing to be ashamed of. He's learning about something people do naturally. If you walked in a room and two little kids were in bed kissing and hugging and rolling around buggin', that would just be what they were doing. Nothing is evil about their actions. They are just doing what people instinctively do. But if an adult exploits this innocence by taking a picture for his own turn-on, he's crossed a line. The kids are not old enough to determine whether or not they want their picture taken. This is really a form of child abuse or child molestation.

If a kid watches a porn film, what is it really going to do to him? It might make him a bold little kid in school, who

■ **"Yo, Pops, that shit you talking is noise.**
■ **Word, you full of shit."**

could probably talk crazy. But all it's really doing is allowing their natural curiosity an outlet.

My daughter used to listen to 2 Live Crew when she was young, and I'd ask her, "What do you like about it? Do you know what they are saying?" And she'd say, "Daddy, they're just talking nasty. I know what that is." What I've done is engage my daughter in conversation and communication, which is more important than saying, "Don't listen to it." If I took that approach, she'd just put the headphones on and listen to it on her own, without my guidance.

There is no way to control life. The worst thing you can do to a kid is try to suppress his or her natural tendencies. Any psychologist will tell you suppression or repression is a breeding ground for what they call dysfunction. If you don't let your kid play with toy guns or watch TV, that boy is going to be sneaking off every chance he gets to his friends' houses looking for some other outlet.

The worst harm that can happen to a child comes directly from the parents, not through music or TV. Really aggressive kids are usually getting the shit beat out of them at home, they're not getting pushy from watching *Teenage Mutant Ninja Turtles*.

I've watched *Friday the 13th* and *A Nightmare on Elm Street* a hundred times, and I'm not about to stab anybody. I listen to Black Sabbath all day, and I don't perform Satanic rituals. If you can make people kill with records, movies, or TV, then news junkies would be out slaying people all day long.

There is no proof 2 Live Crew caused teen pregnancies. These are just smokescreens the opponents to the information exchange throw up. The best way to make people afraid of something is to say, "It'll hurt the children." If I had my own car company and I wanted to put Toyota out of business, the

■ Check this out, Moms, I said time bomb,
■ And they sit in your house and remain calm.

92

best way I could do it was to say more kids got killed in Toyotas.

The children will be all right. Children grow up in the shitstorm of life, and they all pull through unless a parent or somebody who they truly love and respect fucks with them. Absolutely nothing can substitute for parental guidance and love.

That's my opinion on sex, who gives a fuck.

■ Till you feed 'em lies and they flip.
■ Start talking crazy shit.

93

5
Rap: The Art of Shit Talkin'

The main misinterpretation and misunderstanding of rap is in the dialogue—in the ghetto talk and machismo, even in the basic body language. This is what I call shit talkin'. From the nasty tales of Stagolee in the 1800s to H. Rap Brown in the '60s, most of rap is nothing more than straight-up black bravado. Too many people take shit talkin' seriously because they have no frame of reference.

In the ghetto, a black man will say, "I'll take my dick and wrap it around this room three times and fuck yo' mama." Now, this man cannot wrap his dick around the room three times, and he probably doesn't want to fuck your mother, but this is how he's gonna talk to another brother. It's a black thang. It's machismo. It doesn't mean anything.

I rap about my life, and I rap about it in the hardest, most blatant sense.

■ **Fuck you! Might call you and Pops a fool,**

94

When I first started rapping I learned very quickly the political approach couldn't hold a guy's attention, but if I started telling a nasty story, then the audience would really listen. This is no big revelation; sex is used a lot in advertising and the media use it to keep viewers watching until the end of a broadcast. If they advertise "Bikini Stewardesses" at the top of the news, you'll keep watching for a half an hour till they flash the flesh. The media are the worst offenders because when they say, "Oh, look at this. Isn't this awful?" what they are really saying is, "Look at this, look at this, look at this. . . ." All over town sex is used as a teaser to make people go out and pay $7.50 for a movie.

With rap, you quickly learn the trick that you'll get the interest of the audience with sex because they want to know what will happen at the end of the song. They want to see how far I'm gonna take it. If I got onstage and said, "Yeah, I was eating this girl the other night and her pussy tasted like strawberries," everybody in the club would think, "Hooo, shit! This muthafucka's bold." I would get *everybody's* attention and then they would want to know where I could possibly go from there.

The rappers who can hold your attention are either bragging or lying, and most of the stories are lies because if rappers played the moves they talked about—goddamn, they wouldn't have any dicks left.

The art of shit talkin' is responsible for me getting out of crime and getting into rhyme. The best way for me to explain my point of view on hip-hop and its influence on the general public is to give you a brief history of "Ice T the Rapper."

Rapping is just something you pick up growing up in the ghetto. I knew how to write rhymes, because I used to recite rhymes for the gangs. I used to tag, "Crips don't die,

■ Tell ya that's why they hate school.

they multiply." You've probably heard Bebe's Kids use that phrase. I wrote that slogan, and I'm still waiting for my royalty check.

In the gang, I'd write these slogans on the walls, but they were more hustler-style rhymes. When I heard the record "Rapper's Delight," I thought, "Shit, I can do this." And I tried to rap, but I really wasn't particularly good.

We'd go into this club in L.A. called the Radio, and I would try to rap. The reason I kept trying to rap was my boys. They told me to go rap so we could go to the clubs and get some pussy. Once you'd get onstage, the girls would come at you and talk to you. This would be your opportunity to lie and tell 'em you had a record deal. When the film *Breakin'* hit, the director came into the club and told everybody, "Okay, you're gonna be my rapper, you're gonna be my deejay, and you're gonna be my breakers. And I'm going to exploit y'all and make a lot of money."

Now, you've seen that film and that shit was wack. But all y'all know when it came out you were on that shit, "Shabba Doo, yeah." You know you dug it.

So if I was wack, y'all were wack, too.

The movie stylists dressed me up in what they thought breakers and rappers were supposed to wear—things like belts around your crotch and spiked bracelets. I didn't really understand it, and I really didn't want to be in a movie. I didn't have time to be in a movie. The producer told me I was gonna make $500 a day. I told him, "I spend that on sneakers, man."

I did the movie. I tried to rap like New York rappers. I was trying to rap about house parties. "I'll rock the mic, I'll rock the mic, I'll rock the mic." My buddies were all laughing. They would say to me, "Ice, how are you gonna rap about rocking the house parties? We rob parties, man. We're the

■ Been offensive and asking questions
■ Give your brain indigestion.

niggers who come in and say, 'Throw your hands in the air, and leave 'em there.' "

They were right. Nobody was gonna believe it if I didn't rap about the shit I knew. So I wrote this record called "Six in the Morning" about a kid who ran from the police:

Six in the morning, police at my door
Fresh Adidas squeak across the bathroom
**   floor.**

This song was the beginning of what is now called gangsta rap. I call it reality-based rap, because I used real situations and brought them onto the records. I didn't even think of it as gangsta rap, because I thought of myself as a player. I thought I had a little bit more finesse than the gangsters. I still do.

Then, I recorded "Six in the Morning," and everybody liked it. I came up to the Oakland area, and it was pumping all over the place. I knew I had the ability to do this, and my friends encouraged me. It was like if you get up every morning and cook eggs and somebody told you, "You should sell them eggs, man." People told me, "You can sell that rap." "I could do this all day," I thought. "This is easy. This is just about my life."

That's what I've been doing for a while now. I rap about my life, and I rap about it in the hardest, most blatant sense. I consider what I say as real. This is the way the world I come from is. This is the way I talk and I live. This is the only way I can be.

It took me five years from the release of the "Six in the Morning" single to get an album. For those of you who want to get in the rap business, be patient. It takes a while. Finally, I found Warner Brothers, Sire Records. A man named Sey-

Why? Why? Because I have indoctrinated the youth.
They're mentally intoxicated with truth.

mour Stein signed me. When he called me into his office to meet with him, he was playing calypso music and dancing around in his socks. He asked me if I understood calypso music. I told him no. He quickly went into an explanation of calypso and said, "Just because you don't understand what it means doesn't make it invalid. It just means you don't understand. Just the way I might not understand what you're rapping about, it doesn't make it invalid. So go make your album. I know you know what you're talking about."

He told me I was like the Bob Dylan of the streets. And I knew who Bob Dylan was, so I took that as a compliment, even though I thought he was a little crazy. We made the album *Rhyme Pays,* and then Warner Brothers came to me at the label and said they wanted to put a sticker on the record. I asked why. They explained it was to inform the public some material on the album might offend listeners.

I said, "Fine, that's cool." Then they explained to me the organization behind the stickering was called the Parents' Music Resource Center—the PMRC. I thought, "What a nice organization, what a nice name." Little did I know it was founded and headed by this crazed bitch named Tipper Gore, who has made it her job to put down nearly every artist in the music industry for saying what's on their minds. Gore and the PMRC are wholeheartedly against information exchange. Tipper Gore is the only woman I ever directly called a bitch on any of my records, and I meant that in the most negative sense of the word.

Without her help, the album went gold. No video. No radio. My next album, *Power,* featured the cover photo of my girlfriend in a bikini, which everybody looked at longer than they listened to the album. That went gold and so did my third album, *Freedom of Speech . . . Just Watch What You Say.* The next one, *Original Gangster,* had twenty-eight tracks and really was a double album. By this time, a lot of rappers

■ **So they know the noise you talk are lies.**

98

had started rapping these quick little commercials and calling them songs.

"Yo, what's up?"

"Blam. Blam."

That's two songs, right there. So I didn't get credit for a double album, but the album featured twenty-four complete songs.

After *Original Gangster,* we were really rolling, so we decided to go all out and come out with this group called Body Count. Now Body Count, for those of you who aren't slaves to the press, is a rock group, not a rap group. Body Count was created because I like rock music. I didn't know I wasn't supposed to like rock music. I've been listening to rock music my whole life—Black Sabbath, Blue Oyster Cult, Deep Purple, Black Flag, Circle Jerks, X. I moved into Minor Threat. I listened to No Means No, Cannibal Corpse, Gwar. I was into this whole shit. I liked rock because I like the rage I got out of it. I found rage in Slayer and Megadeth, and used that same rage to make my music.

Everybody should know rock 'n' roll was really started by black artists like Little Richard, who raged on the piano. The music executives then stepped in and had Pat Boone remake all his records. And they decided: White people can rock and black people will do R & B. That's the biggest joke; rock is a state of mind, not a question of color. If you sing about love, and going to school, and drinking milkshakes, and having sex in the missionary position, you're doing pop music. Pop music means popular music. You're attempting to be popular.

The problem with pop is what's popular today will not be popular tomorrow. Talk to Tone Lōc about that shit. Tone is my friend, but he knows he was on some pop shit. "Wild Thing" blew up because it became popular, but now he has to build a core audience, which I know he can do because

■ Pretty damn soon they'll be by, I'm outta here.

the man has talent. Your core audience is what's important. Your core audience will buy your records without hearing a single. If you love Prince, and he has an album out, you'll buy that album. You don't wait to hear a song. You just buy Prince. That's your core audience; they don't have to see the video, they just wait until the record's out, and they buy it immediately.

With "Body Count," I knew we didn't want to form an R & B group. To me, R & B goes something like this:

> **Baby don't leave me,**
> **But if you do leave me,**
> **Don't take the car.**
> **And if you do take that car,**
> **Shake that ass on the**
> **Way out the door.**

That's cool music, but where am I gonna get the rage and the anger to attack something with that? Back in the '60s, you had Stevie Wonder and Marvin Gaye, and they were putting out powerful music. Now, it's just "Shake that ass. Shake that ass. Shake that ass."

We knew Body Count had to be a rock band. The name alone negates the band from being R & B. We named the group Body Count because every Sunday night in L.A., I'd watch the news, and the newscasters would tally up the youths killed in gang homicides that week and then just segue to sports. "Is that all I am," I thought, "a body count?"

I ended up being Body Count's lead singer by default. I knew I couldn't sing, but then I thought, "Who *can* sing in rock 'n' roll?" Fuck that. I'm the singer. If you listen to death metal, you don't even know what they're singing. It all sounds

■ They listen to me and I give 'em the real.

like "ARGGGGGGGGGGGGGGGGGGGGGGGGGGGGGG-GGGGGGG!" I figured I could do that.

I don't play an instrument, but to me writing music is easy and comes naturally. Most of the best songwriters out there don't even play instruments. And just because you can play an instrument doesn't mean you can write any songs. So all y'all who are good hummers can write songs.

I scored the music and wrote the lyrics for the album with Ernie C., the lead guitarist. We went on tours and people dug us. Little did I know the song titled "Cop Killer" was gonna cause the country to go nuclear. I didn't even think "Cop Killer" was a controversial record, because everybody I know hates the cops. I thought everybody hated the police. And I thought all my fans hate the police—they liked the record, didn't they? Through the "Cop Killer" event, I learned who was really on whose side.

In between the forming of Body Count and the "Cop Killer" explosion, I moved over to feature films. I did *New Jack City, Ricochet,* and *Trespass* back to back.

There must not be enough young black actors, because directors invite rappers to be in their films. Although we are already used to getting onstage and performing, I for one have absolutely no idea how to really act. I would read a script that tells me to say, "Open the door." So I would say, "Open the door." And the director would flip, "Unbelievable." I thought, "This shit is easy, too. I could do this."

One of the most traumatic things in my life was taking the role in *New Jack City.* When Mario Van Peebles asked me to be in his film, I thought he was joking when he stepped up to me in a club. I was just chillin', hanging out with some ladies, and I thought he really just wanted to meet the women. "Yeah, right, you want me to be in your film, you

■ **And every night a cap gets peeled,**

just want to get one of these girls. This is Michelle and this is . . ."

The next day he called me and invited me to come to the Warners lot. So I drove to Warner Brothers, and the producers told me:

"We've got this part. It's perfect for you. It was written for you."

"Really? Okay, what's the part?"

"A policeman."

"A policeman?"

"Yeah, but with dreadlocks."

"Do I got to own slaves, too?"

I was not into doing this film. I've seen too many rappers get into the music business, then try to make a movie and go out. Everybody's not *Tougher Than Leather*. Go ask Run–D.M.C. whether they went out on *Tougher Than Leather*. They'll tell you that shit was wack. I would never dis Run–D.M.C., they are two of the greatest rappers ever, but they know D.M.C. can't hit no cop in the face and walk away.

Shit, I knew *Breakin'* was waaaaaaack, and I wasn't about to fuck up again. I wanted to work with Mario, but I just couldn't play a cop. I didn't know what to do. Mario and the producers wanted me to play a policeman, and I was scared. "My fans are gonna hate this," I thought. So I went to my buddies. "They want me to be in a movie," I said. "They want me to play a policeman."

My buddies said, "Word? Can I be in the movie?"

None of them told me not to do it.

Then I called my homies in the penitentiary. Whenever I really need something, I talk to my boys locked down. "What do you think about this? They want me to be in this movie, but they want me to play a policeman."

■ And every night a ho gets smacked, a fool gets jacked.

They said, "Word? If I was out, could I be in the movie?"

I was like, fuck y'all. When I really need an answer, I go talk to women. They asked me, "Well, is he a good cop?"

"Yeah."

"Then no problem."

So I acted in the movie.

All these opportunities opened up for me because I could do something every kid in the ghetto learns at one point or another. I could talk shit. And I got paid for it. Society really wasn't ready for people like me to make it into the mainstream.

When I originally began rapping, I rapped for a very specific audience. When my albums started to move, and the corporation started making money off us, a lot of new people tuned in who weren't really ready to hear it. My favorite faction—the watchdogs of the profane—moved in and completely flipped.

Rap is very funny music, but if you don't understand the humor, it will scare the shit out of you. Taken literally, the music is so over the top it offends your sensibilities. But within my community, rap is verbal combat. We get around a lot of fights and aggression simply by talking. The misinterpretation of rap comes from people who have no insight into the ghetto mentality and attitude.

Black people—and I mean poor black people, because usually the lower you are economically the more people you live around—project a "fuck you" attitude. When you have less economically, you're around more people and you get deeper into your culture and ethnicity. Black people on this particular level talk shit. We, as a race, run our mouth. We

■ Now, whose fucking fault was that?
■ The home invaders.

talk a lot about each other's mother, and we talk about each other's head.

When rap first hit the scene, in the ghetto it was really role-model music because it uplifted the community to feel we finally had a chance to be heard. It became our means of information exchange from ghetto to ghetto, from city to city. New York kids never knew about L.A. kids and Texas kids. Now, with rap, we talked, we communicated.

We all talked in the language of the ghetto. A rapper uses this language just to maintain his integrity. I am not a pop star; I do not write pop records. I am from South Central Los Angeles. I use the word "nigger." I use the word "bitch." That's how I talk, and that's how my audience talks.

Take a listen to the song, "99 Problems and a Bitch Ain't One," off my *Home Invasion* album. Change the word "bitch" to "girl" and it's a pop record, not a street record. "Bitch" equals street. "Girl" equals pop. I can sell that one to Vanilla Ice. Now it's a singsongy Beach Boys tune: "I got a girl from the east, I got a girl from the west." It'll be good for a few laughs. But this is not who I am. I use words like "bitch" and "nigger" and "fuck," and my audience doesn't expect me to be any different.

I'm not saying that's where it ends. I'm saying that's where it is. My records are directed at very hard people. These are brothers in the streets who ain't listening to nobody. It takes unconventional tactics to keep these brothers listening. So the aggressiveness is the only way I could keep this audience tuned in. If I tried to adopt a golly-gee white dialect, everybody would think I'd lost my mind.

We have very different definitions of words. For example, I don't have a problem with the word "nigger." Early on, it was only used as a derogatory term for a black person. You had the "house niggers" and the "field niggers." The house nigger would be the one who was inside making the beds,

■ **"Yo! Yo! Yo! All that shit you taught me, Mom, was full of shit,**

cooking the food, kissing ass. The field nigger was in the field fuckin' shit up. They wouldn't conform. They were the real niggers. I wear that term like a badge of honor. If some square Tom politician is not a nigger, then I *am* a nigger, you understand? I am not what you want me to be. I'm the worst side of it. The field niggers are my niggers.

In ghetto dialect, we'll call white people niggers. It doesn't mean color. In my song "Straight Up Nigga," I went through a lot of uses for the word. But when the white dude on the album says, "Look at those niggers," we don't play that shit. With every one of these words, the definition boils down to its real context.

I can talk shit all night with my female friends, and they don't even get involved. They don't play that. A so-called feminist will never understand the song "99 Problems." First off, they can't get over the word "bitch." They'll trip over it forever. If a white man calls a white woman a bitch in his house, she shivers, she shakes, her head spins around like Linda Blair's in *The Exorcist*.

The word "bitch" from the ghetto perspective is a non-gender-specific slang term for anybody who thinks the world revolves around them. It can also be used as an endearment. A guy will call the woman he loves, would never leave, would die for, his bitch. But don't *you* ever call her a bitch.

"Yo, my bitch was tripping. . . ."

"You need to check your bitch."

"Who the fuck you calling a bitch?"

A black girl, on the other hand, will say, "Yeah, I'm a bitch. Straight up." Shit talkin' doesn't piss off ghetto women, 'cause anything I can issue to a ghetto girl she's got an answer for. They'll answer all the shit we talk with a "Fuck you, Ice." And that's it. They don't say. "You're sexist." They respond with their own rap, something like:

■ **Know what I'm saying?**

105

**All these bitches you
talkin' 'bout you fuckin', nigga,
you ain't gettin' no pussy.
You got a little dick,
and you talking all that shit.
That's 'cause you ain't shit, nigga.**

Check out the girl version of shit talkin', the album by Bytches with Problems. They stick it to us hard. Girls love it, but I can't listen to it. The shit scares me. By the same token, if women don't want to listen to me or Cube, they'll just turn it off.

A lot of rappers use this verbal combat against women early on in the game because they are suspicious. For many of them, this is the first time they've ever had girls approach them. All of a sudden, white women, black women, you name it, want to get with a brother who couldn't have gotten sex, let alone a date, with a woman a few months earlier.

Now, a successful rapper, they've got money, and they've really got an attitude. Through their music, they vent some of their anger. They don't hate women, but for the first time in their lives, probably, they got women approaching them. "What the fuck is up? Why do you like me?" I'm looking at this gorgeous girl hanging over Biz Markie, and she's telling Biz Markie she thinks he's the cutest guy she's ever seen. And Biz Markie knows he ain't cute. He may be fly, but she's pushing it. Biz is thinking, "Fuck you, bitch. What the fuck are you doing?"

A lot of people will never understand a rapper's point of view. Why they'll voluntarily allow themselves to be offended as they listen to the shit for hours I'll never understand. With rap, you're basically eavesdropping on a phone conversation between two buddies. When white America picks

■ How the fuck you gonna tell me to run my muthafuckin' life?

106

up the phone, they say, "Gosh! Why do you talk like that?" And we answer, "Because we're talking to each other. This is how we talk. If you don't like it, hang up the fuckin' phone." You can always turn the record off. If you listened to the entire record, and you allowed yourself to be provoked, then who's the fool now?

I've never understood the word "profanity." At each lecture I gave around the country at college campuses, I would ask the people in the audience to define the term to me. Nobody could do it. These were Ivy League kids at Ivy League colleges. If you look up profanity in the dictionary, the word is defined as "something blasphemous." If you look up blasphemy, it's defined as "irreverence." I challenge anybody to tell me how the word "shit" is going to send me to hell.

When your parents use the word "goddamn," they are using it as an exclamation point to bring attention to a sentence or a word. There is a distinct difference between your mother saying, "Don't use the car," and your father saying, "Don't use the goddamn car." He is using a taboo word in order to draw attention to the sentence to emphasize his point. He didn't mean to slam God. He just meant business when he told you not to use the car.

I find all the people who oppose profanity extremely ignorant, because the words they don't like they can't even define. Until somebody can explain to me why I shouldn't use certain words, I will continue to use them. I challenge anybody who reads this book to write an honest evaluation of profanity.

The closer you look at the hypocrisies involved in the use or disuse of profanity, the more amusing they get. Slang words are against the law. You've got kids dying in the street every night, but nobody's policing that mess. This country

■ Bitch! You don't even know who the fuck you are

107

has "slang police." According to the FCC, you can't say "tit" on the radio, but you can say "boob." You can't say "dick," but you can say "penis." Now what's that about?

MTV runs ads telling you to vote and to fight for your rights, but these "slang police" routinely censor their videos. They bleep out words and censor images. You have to find out in advance if your video will offend them, because if it does, they won't air it. They won't air the word "nigger." So when I did the video for Body Count's "There Goes the Neighborhood," the word "nigger" had to be changed to "black boy." Doing that alters the strength and meaning of the song. I've already come to the conclusion there is no free speech in America, though. I've already concluded that 99 percent of the idiots on the planet are running this world, and I have to deal with it. So I'm not even gonna let them trip me out.

Every hardcore rap artist has been censored at one point or another. That's just the way it is. People don't talk about it, but it's been going on since the beginning. Entire songs get pulled off albums before they are released, words have to be rewritten or are bleeped out. Passages of songs will be quietly dropped in the pressing stage. Artwork gets destroyed. An artist is forced to write a "clean" version of a "dirty" song. The list goes on and on. At one point or another, every rap artist has had to make compromises. But it doesn't really even matter to me anymore, because I realized a long time ago that censorship is as American a tradition as apple pie.

Every artist in America who is even slightly political, or who doesn't see the world like Pat Boone, has endured some form of censorship. In every art form, from straight painting to music, dance, and ballet, the artists have to deal with the censors. The Jesse Helmses come out of the woodwork and say, "Those two women can't kiss in that picture. He can't have a bullwhip up his butt in that photograph. Is that urine

■ You talking about you don't like rap, you don't like how I dress

flying toward that crucifix? Look, America, look America, look, look, look, look. . . ."

My definition of art is anything which has required skill to create. Everybody out here who has a skill and has practiced it has dealt with somebody who tells them, "You can't do that. You can't do that. You can't say that. You can't write that. You can't think that."

Okay, everybody, let's just admit there is censorship. Let's quit pretending. Anybody who says, "Oh, we don't censor," is the biggest liar around. Everything is censored, except maybe what you say in the privacy of your home, and they'd love to get in there. Even sexual activities are restricted in your own house, in your own bedroom. Certain sex acts are actually illegal in some states. We live in a censored environment controlled by the law. Every night, people break laws in the privacy of their own homes.

I personally appreciate all the work and effort my self-proclaimed enemies put into fighting what I do. If something makes me mad, it gives me something to rap about. That's what hardcore rap is all about, rapping about problems. I rap about problems.

Whenever anybody in the past has asked me why I use the word "bitch," I have explained to them that bitches are a problem for me. I don't rap about positive women or men, because positive women and men aren't a problem. There are other rappers who rap about the positive, and that's cool, because that's who they are. But that's not who I am. Put it this way, if I were a movie director, all I would focus on were killers. If somebody asked me to make films about positive men, I'd tell them I couldn't possibly do that because I make films about men who murder. Why would anybody step to Stephen King and tell him he should be writing books and

◀ Yo! Fuck you and Pops
◀ I'm outta here both of y'all can kiss my ass."

making movies like *Fried Green Tomatoes?* Stephen King writes about the dark side of life and so do I. The only difference is I don't make up my subjects.

Because I write about the real things I see, I am perceived as irresponsible. People argue, "You're telling kids to treat people in a negative manner." They are worried about some effect a particular record of mine is going to have on children, and I don't see it. Every study debunks the theory that people murder or rape because they watch it on TV or hear it on a record. That kid is usually seriously disturbed because he's raised by fucked-up parents. Put those parents on trial, not the record. Rock 'n' roll may make me want to drive my car fast, but really, I already want to drive my car fast. The music is just a good accompaniment to speed.

The cops were salivating during the "Cop Killer" controversy, because they wanted to pin a murder on me. They were really disappointed that Ronald Ray Howard, the nineteen-year-old kid from Texas who shot a cop, wasn't listening to Body Count. He was supposedly listening to Tupac Shakur's *2PACOLYPSE NOW*, which addresses cop killing.

I talked to Tupac recently, and he knows that's all one big con. What are the courts gonna do, have a new law on the books where the court says you're innocent by reason of musical insanity? The irony is the cops originally said the record causes you to create violence, but they wanted this kid so bad, they fought against it, saying the record didn't cause him to do it because they wanted him to fry. They didn't want the record involved anymore.

Originally, they were trying to set a precedent in court proving a record can make you murder. But now that the court found the record was not responsible, it will forever stick in court. It's stuck. They can't pull any more stunts.

So they wanted Ronald Ray Howard. They were so bloodthirsty for this kid that once they got him, it created a

■ All cops want me, so does the F.B.I.
■ Because my rhymes are fly.

ruling that murderers are responsible for their own actions. Now, if they had found the record company guilty of conspiracy, cops would be running around totally scared. Records do not make people kill. Maybe this record was just good background music for a kid who already had every reason to hate cops. That's what these records are about. They tell people, "Hey, listen up, these kids hate cops because these cops have been fucking with them for too long."

I talked to Cube about the kid, and he said, "Fuck that kid. That kid knows what he's doing. He knows he's trying to pull the record company in. He did the murdering. Fuck him."

He pulled the trigger. What about the kids who shot each other playing Nintendo? One kid said the killer used to tell other kids to call him Rambo. So how come Stallone wasn't taken to court over this little kid? They're never gonna do that; they're just gonna fuck with rap records or rock records. Anything that is punk, they'll fuck with.

When I came out with the *Power* album, cops took pictures of kids laid out in the street with my tape in their pockets. Cops will do whatever they can to make the association. But don't be misled; Ronald Ray Howard had an entirely different reason for smoking that cop. Maybe he didn't want to come. Maybe he didn't like cops. Maybe he was fed up. He definitely didn't want to go to jail. He just said, "Fuck it. It's on." A person who will kill a cop after listening to a record is already unstable. If that's the case, you better keep dinner forks out of their hands too!

That's just my opinion on rap, who gives a fuck.

■ **They still trying to stop me shut me down, block me.**
■ **Make muthafuckas boycott me.**

6
Religion: One Percent Nation

When I first moved from New Jersey to Los Angeles, I was sent to live with a religious aunt of mine. She was a Sunday-school teacher, and each week she would take me to "Christ Church." I was twelve years old, and I was already suspicious. It seemed to me that none of the Christian religions practiced in America were really made to include the black community. Whatever the first blacks saw when they got off the boat was not designed for them or for Indians or Asians or anybody who wasn't a white Christian. Churches and religion were designed to help the white people who were already there to maintain control.

I became even more suspicious of the church when I was out on the streets. People were living in such poverty, and all the praying in the

It's a man's ques
to be God. Or at
least his best
friend.

■ But that will never happen. It's impossible.

world didn't seem to be helping their situation. When I began to have really hard times out on the street, I stopped going to church altogether. I was damn near on a homeless tip when I was in my twenties. I was hustling, and I didn't have an apartment. I was staying either in hotels or at a buddy's house.

When I was rolling, I'd have a career for two months, then I'd flip and move, and there were times when I was extremely broke; I wound up spending a lot of time alone. When I got hurt and went through trauma, I knew I had a choice. I could either pray or not pray. I decided I wasn't going to pray.

When you're out on the streets, after a while you start realizing it's gonna be only you. You're going to have to look after yourself. No one else is gonna take care of you.

When I was doing wrong, I thought of it as a jinx to pray. If I had prayed to get away with a wrong, I would probably have gone under. Rather than calling God in to help me do low, I thought I'd better try to do it where he won't see me.

A car accident twelve years ago really changed my outlook on spirituality. I woke up in a hospital with a priest sitting beside me. He was going through some religious rites, and I yelled, "Get him away from me!" It's not that I didn't want his help, but at that point I didn't feel like I wanted to pray for anything. I had never used an outside person for help or an outside religion for relief. I was afraid to. They told me I'd never walk again, so I went into myself and pulled myself together the only way I knew how. Alone.

I didn't want to rely on prayer and think that it alone was gonna make me get better. I didn't trust it. "I *have* to get better," I told myself. I refused to pray. I just went right into myself. I learned that no religion is more powerful than

■ **I move straight through all obstacles.**

your own spirit and determination. This became the main philosophy of the One Percent Nation, my current belief system.

I formed the One Percent Nation with members of my crew on the Lollapalooza tour in '91, and it quickly became a way of life for me. The main premise is that one percent of the world doesn't wait to seek out heaven in the afterlife; we strive for it now. We're not suckered in by religions that offer death payoffs; we already know how to find happiness and how to live in love in *this* lifetime.

One-Percenters see the ideals of the Nation more as a living theory than a religion because we don't pray to an icon. We believe that heaven and hell are emotional states, not real places you're sent to when you die. As a One-Percenter, you believe the worst hell you can ever possibly be in is when you're emotionally hurt, when somebody you love abandons you or a member of your family dies and the loss leaves you with a broken heart.

Although I've been through serious physical pain—the car accident left my pelvis broken in three places—I learned that no amount of physical pain can compare to the hurt in your heart. No happiness can compare to the joy you feel when you are around people you love or your partner is making you feel good—not just physically, but spiritually. These feelings put you in touch with heaven, and One-Percenters seek out the positive emotional state of heaven.

Humans can launch a rocket ship from earth that will land on a planet in fifty years, but they cannot create a living cell from scratch. Only God, a force that is neither male nor female, has the power to create the miracle of life. One-Percenters believe the creation of life is the most important element of existence. Sex is the only thing you're going to do in life that is holy, because this is where you create life. Every-

■ They say I'm fucking up the minds of little kids,

114

thing else you do should be a quest to make the world better for other people and the lives of children.

We've been compared to a sex cult because we believe the meaning of life—the Holy Grail—is found in the male and female connection, in reproduction. If God didn't want us to make love, sex would be the most distasteful, terrible thing in the world. If we had to slash our own wrists to have children, we wouldn't have any children. We would be extinct.

Instead, the act of love is an act of euphoria. Without drugs, without any stimulant, sex allows you to travel through time or space. When the connection is really intense, you actually leave your body and travel through time and when you finish, you come slowly back to earth. I'm convinced sex is the ultimate drug.

There is no doubt in my mind that when it comes to sex, 99 percent of the world is frustrated. One-Percenters believe you can have as many sexual partners or lovers as your heart can handle. We feel your heart is a meter, a conscience, that lets you know when you're doing something wrong. Your heart dictates when you've had enough. In the Muslim religion, a man can have as many wives as he can take care of, and we feel a man or a woman can have as many lovers as they can love.

A woman might feel she can only love one person, and if she tries to be with another guy, she won't be able to love them both. Then monogamy is right for her. Another woman might be able to love two men at once, and that's what's right for her. Most people who think like the second woman have society's guilt imposed on them.

Something's wrong with this second picture. They are allowing the rules of these other religions to control their impulses. These impulses should be dictated from your heart to your head. Denying your human instincts is unnatural, and

■ But half my fans are in college. ■ PMRC suck my dick, please.
■ You can kiss my ass while you're on your knees. Word!
115

it's this type of suppression that leads to frustration. Frustration causes people to act out.

Following your instincts doesn't always mean you're going to be reckless about your desires. A One-Percenter has to make sure his or her partner understands the philosophy first. Let your partner know up front you aren't necessarily gonna be monogamous. If your partner can't deal with that, then you can't deal with them. A One-Percenter understands sex isn't about control.

One-Percenters' beliefs have evolved since the sexual revolution. We understand the era in which we live demands safe sex and responsibility. Our only sin is bringing unwanted babies into the world. Creating children is the only holy thing you're ever gonna do. It has to be taken seriously. When you and a partner decide you're going to bring a child into this world, this is your ultimate task. This is *it*. You're not ever gonna do anything comparable to bringing a life into the world.

You can bring records in all day, movies, big shit. But a baby has to be thought out, preplanned. You don't have to be married, and you don't have to live together, but both parents have to know and understand that this child is *both* their responsibility, and they have to prepare for it. Safe sex and birth control should always be practiced when you're not going into our worship and creating a child.

If you have sex and you're not creating a child, you're still exchanging love, happiness, and good feelings. The sexual act is still something beautiful. You're saying to your partner, "Yo, we can make each other feel good. I think we should do this, so let's travel." It's another way of getting high.

The Christians in this country want to deny this. They turn it into:

■ **You're listening to [reading, ed. sic] the verbal assassinator**

The Big Love Thing
Monogamy
Till Death Do Us Part

We don't believe in these traditional notions of love. We believe passion can overcome love in certain situations. If two people decide to just enjoy each other, then that's cool.

You can't end up at the end of the day saying, "Uh, I want you badly. I have to own you." People don't own each other. That's when negative energy kicks in. That's not the real world. Maybe two people will find each other and want to be together monogamously; it's a natural progression in that case. If it's an unnaturally forced contract, then resentment builds. Forcing love is what leads to The Lie: "I'll be with you forever." If we had enough One-Percenters, there wouldn't be a need for The Lie. Before critics start yelling "Sexism!" the female in the One Percent Nation has just as much right to walk up to a male at any time and say, "Hey, I'm with it. I feel you. I want to be with you." It's entirely possible the man won't be able to handle it. He might tell her he's not ready or he can only love one person or he might decide to go for it. It's all directed by your heart and what you're about.

The "M" word, m-a-r-r-i-a-g-e, should just be a commitment of love, a statement saying, "I love this person. And we're going to be partners." God will, in turn, say, "Good luck, my children. I'm backing you." In the meantime, you have to understand—love is conditional. Whenever somebody says "Forever," they're lying. People love each other as long as they are treated in an appropriate manner. The minute a husband becomes an alcoholic and beats his wife in the head or abuses his children, she shouldn't be thinking "Till death do us part" anymore. *A 99-Percenter created that vow.*

■ 'E's the cross-fader, your factual updater—

God would actually tell her, "I think it's time you go. This dude's gone crazy." Under the contract of marriage, though, she's supposed to stay down. Marriage becomes a smoke-screen that has nothing to do with the love of two people.

I am more or less spiritually married. I love my girl, and we've been together eight years, and we'll continue to be together as long as we keep up with each other's standards. If that doesn't happen, there will be some kind of division. Hopefully, we'll stay together, but why sign off on a binding document that stipulates a situation never changes? The One Percent Nation is simply more realistic in its outlook.

Our slogan is "One Percent Nation, 99 percent frustration." The 99-Percenters are the people who cause all the problems in the world. We consider their religions "middle-man religions." Once you enlist in a middleman religion, you'll be going through some icon—Jesus, Muhammed, the Buddha—to get to God.

Middleman religions are the reason so many people are at war and dying, because they're constantly trying to outrank each other. Muslims will fight Jews, and Christians will fight Muslims. All they're doing is fighting to be the middleman. One group will convince you to go with them, "We'll get you MCI to God." Another says, "Nah, nah, nah. We'll get you Sprint."

God doesn't discriminate. God speaks to every person because every person is a miracle. No child is farther from God or the power than the next person. The pope doesn't outrank anybody, you dig? The pope doesn't outrank you or me. We all can get in touch with the power. Every life is of equal value and has an equal connection to the power and it has nothing to do with race or sex or how much money you send the fuckin' church.

Unfortunately, 99 percent of the people live off middle-man religions that rely on death payoffs: "If you be good,

■ **Until your cranium grows,** ■ **Like uranium, hard as titanium** you'll go to heaven. If you're bad, you'll burn in hell. Now give me your money, and I'll save you."

If I could run a business that pays off when you die, I'd be a rich muthafucka because nobody could come back for a refund. And middleman religions *are* big business.

In the One Percent Nation, you don't have to wait until death to find heaven, because you live it now. I live in heaven at this moment, but it takes sincere effort. You begin by eliminating miserable people from your life. Miserable people love company, and 99 percent of the world will always be uptight. When you encounter a 99-Percenter, you offer them an opportunity to be a One-Percenter by trying to help him solve his problem. You tell him, "Look, homey, you need to go find a girl and get someone who cares about you and mellow out and eliminate all these negative people around you. You'll be happier." Or at least get him around his mother or somebody who cares about him—it doesn't necessarily have to be sexual, it could be another guy, it don't matter. You simply need to be with somebody who makes you happy.

If your buddy continues to hang around the 99-Percenters, he's going to live in hell the rest of his life, and he'll try to take you in there, too. A clever One-Percenter can really understand when someone is trying to take him into hell. When your woman or your man starts up, it's your job to say, "Mellow out, I'll try to help you deal with the problem, but don't bring me in there. I'm not going in there with you."

One-Percenters feel two of the most important things in life are your health and your freedom. Everything else is an accessory. If you're not free, you're living in hell. We believe you try to stay out of the negative emotional states by being a good person. We believe in karma, in reaping what you sow. If you give out positive vibes, you'll receive positive energy. If you give out negativity, expect to suffer the consequences.

◀ Parents I'm blamin 'em—
◀ For teaching you lies about life,

Although the One Percent Nation is on the yin-yang system, incorporating elements of Buddhism, Hinduism, the *Kama Sutra*, and Thoreau's teachings, we don't adhere strictly to any other morals or any rules set up by existing religions. We understand the rules and the laws issued by the 99 percent who are uptight about their sexuality or have a need to control. They're living in the world of the 99-Percenters, and they will issue their own judgments. If you don't play by their rules, they will attempt to create hell for you and take away your freedom.

One-Percenters understand that we live in a world of fools and we can't make the laws, but we don't necessarily abide by them entirely. We understand if a man goes out and kills another man, God will issue a penalty for him. But 99-Percenters feel they have to go attack and seek retribution. We ain't with that.

The irony behind the One Percent Nation is that on the surface it appears to go against so many of society's rules but it's actually a very practical belief system. We expose sexual taboos and hypocrisies; we understand that 99 percent of the world will never understand us, never agree with us, never take this in. In many ways, we are much less sensational than most Catholics and fundamentalists. They condemn homosexuality and birth control and abortion; we don't. We understand homosexuality exists, people should always practice safe sex, and the biggest crime of all is unwanted babies.

Although the world is run by 99-Percenters, there will always be people who are One-Percenters—whether they know it or not—who already live by these guidelines. I have spoken about and understand the hypocrisy of the 99 percent. These people don't name their religion, they just reach for peace. They are the One Percent.

The One Percent Nation can run in conjunction with any religion you might already embrace. You can be a Baptist

■ **Racist viewpoints and other trite bullshit**
■ **They learned back in the day**

and still have One Percent ideology. Guys in my crew are extremely religious. My buddy Patrone puts gospel music on his Walkman when we go on planes, and he doesn't take those headphones off till we land. He says he wants to be talking to God the whole time he's flying, because if the plane starts to crash, he's already got God's ear. He doesn't want the line to be busy.

Even though my buddies include six guys who follow variations of Islam, two Christians, and three guys who actually go to church, almost all of them have transferred their spirituality to the One Percent Nation. We have to be One-Percenters in order not to argue with each other. All we really got is each other, and we know it.

We never say to anyone, "Lose your other religion and join us." This makes people stop relying on their religions on their own initiative; compared to the One Percent Nation, most other religions are too restrictive, too full of denial and condemnation.

Although the Five Percent Nation—a Muslim-based religion popular in the world of hip-hop—is similar in ideology to the One Percent Nation, it has some variations I don't agree with. You can't eat certain foods, and a lot of the members are totally against white people. Some believe white people are the devil. Some are anti-Semitic. On the other hand, some members—they call each other gods—will say you should judge the devil by his deeds, and that's closer to our philosophy.

One-Percenters don't have racist beliefs. They believe anything truly good, will not condemn. As soon as the Catholics say, "You're gonna go to hell," right there they lost me. They are trying to issue an ultimatum: "This is how it is." Maybe that's not how it really is. We leave things open for interpretation.

During the "Cop Killer" controversy, I met with Minister

While I learned about death from an AK.

121

Louis Farrakhan in his home in Chicago. I told him, "You know, I'm down with the Muslims, and I understand your religion can be very uplifting, but I can't give up my bacon. And I ain't gonna tell you I wouldn't be with no white women. I'm gonna tell you the truth."

He told me, "Ice, nobody's ever come to my house and talked to me like that. Either you're very crazy. Or you're very powerful. And I'll bet on the second." I have extremely high respect for the minister, and it was a great honor to be invited into his home. He respected my beliefs, and for that alone, I will always look at him as a great man.

With all the anger I express in my records, I still have found a way to get peace. I've either eliminated the 99-Percenters, or at least I see them coming. I don't allow people to raise their voice around me. Everything is cool, everything can be dealt with. I've had to cut off a lot of people because they keep it too intense, they are always unhappy.

A lot of people simply aren't getting any. A lack of love on any level hurts. If you're not getting love from your parents or from a partner, inside you're screaming in pain: *"I'm not getting no girl! I ain't got no money! I'm miserable!"*

I'm willing to think the Los Angeles police probably have some of the most fucked-up sex lives of any occupation. All they do all day is see rich people partying, drug dealers with fine women, rock stars getting laid. They are some of the most frustrated 99-Percenters around.

On a world scale, frustrations over sex and power lead to religious persecution. Religion is like music: It shouldn't be argued. People just believe. Music just exists. Agree with them or move on. Listen or turn it off. Unfortunately, so many of the wars that have been fought have been holy wars—people split not only on racial differences but on religious differences.

■ But they'll never quite understand
■ Bam bam bam no gat is the Walkman

When I was in Britain, and I saw the torture chambers and learned about the Spanish Inquisition and what people went through to be "freed from demons," I thought it was all pure madness. Anybody who can look at those things and not believe that ain't hell in itself doesn't make any sense.

Religious persecution has to end. Religion is something people use to feel good about themselves. It's a spiritual tool. If somebody believes he found salvation in Jesus Christ and Jesus Christ is giving him the strength to make it through each day, fine. That's great. I'm not gonna tell him he didn't find the strength in Jesus Christ because maybe he did.

I'm aware enough to know that I don't know. I'm not condemning anybody's religion. An atheist will say, "If you believe in Jesus, you're crazy, 'cause you're wrong, there ain't no Jesus." But I'm not standing here in judgment, because I might die and when I land on the other side, a gang of Hare Krishnas might just be there chanting, "See?!"

There are men in India sitting on mountains. There are monks living in solitude. All these people are in touch with some spiritual being or force. All these people aren't fools. Indirectly, everybody comes in contact with the same life force. And I'm just trying to deal with it straight up, with my person.

I don't believe in pushing ideals on other people. You have to seek ideals out on your own and learn what works for you. Over time, I've come to consider myself a spiritual person, because I've learned to respect the unknown. When I was hustling, I used to be a very "Fuck him. Fuck her"–type dude. I had to get mine, and I had nothing but problems. Since I turned my life around and started treating people with respect and looking out for people, I've gotten nothing but positive results.

Even the people who went out and did me low didn't really hurt me. They hurt me a different way, because I would

■ Boom, bash yeah yo, it's going down
■ Me and Ice Cube are in town

give out love, and they would turn around and not respect it. I understand a lot of people are still searching for what I found.

In the Bible, Jesus says don't judge a man who knows not what he does. I have learned to look around for people who understand themselves and who don't fear the world. People know when they're stepping out of bounds and doing wrong, and I try to make sure I don't do that. I try to stay within my guidelines.

People are always trying to unsettle you. If you live your life in prayer to some icon and this is what you believe in and how you find hope, why would anybody want to take that away from you? What do I gain by doing that unless I'm a minister, and I'm trying to get you to put money into my church? Or even worse, I'm a political figure and I'm trying to use the Christian doctrine to manipulate you?

Many people are unaware that the United States is run on a very religious, Christian basis. The money reads "In God We Trust," and a lot of the country's laws are religious statutes: ages of consent, bigamy statutes. The country's moral codes are Christian-based. Many of the censorship issues we run into are rooted in religious ideals and prudish notions.

On the flip side, the Constitution says flat out there is supposed to be a separation of church and state. This presents an interesting paradox. Is America a straight-up government that's run by the people or is it run by the principles of the Christian church?

Although the United States mandates that people have religious freedom, the Christian doctrine holds the greatest power. It decides how people should dress, how they should act—especially people in power.

The Southern Christian fundamentalists have a strangle-

124

hold on this country. They throw their weight around a lot. They own the Southern malls, and they step to store managers and threaten to picket their stores when they sell our records. In the store owner's contract, it reads, "If you cause a disturbance in this mall, you could lose your lease." Instead of causing a disturbance, the owners pull the record. That's just a tiny example of the control fundamentalists have in this country.

Although the Christian church in black communities still has an active presence, the primary followers are older black people and parents who still have the slave mentalities. They haven't snapped out of it yet. The kids on the street are banned or self-exiled from the church. If they don't have a mother to bring them into the church, there's really nothing to make them want to go in there. The rules and restrictions of the church are not liberal enough to allow a confused kid a chance to get in.

When the white missionaries came to Africa and the blacks were enslaved, they first instilled the fear of God in us. They used fear against us to keep us enslaved. In America, the Ku Klux Klan was able to scare the shit out of us by dressing up like spooks and burning crosses. Our people felt, "Who on earth could be so diabolical they would burn a cross? Isn't that God?" The Klan scared the shit out of black people.

Today, black Americans are tired of the Jesus Christ image that is perpetuated. Everybody should know that Christ's famous portrait is a picture of Michelangelo's brother. If you read the Bible, the scriptures say the man had woolly hair. Even the region he came from offers overwhelming evidence that he was black.

If they would at least give us that much credit in the church, Christianity might be strengthened. By saying the son

■ What do they do? What did I do?
■ Just say truth muthafucka and it's coming through.

of God is white, that makes God white then. And all this does is compound the feeling in black Americans that they are second-class people.

Right now, the youth is taking Jesus and categorizing him as a wise man or a prophet. With the introduction of hip-hop, a lot of kids are shedding old concepts and exploring totally different ideas.

The whole point behind my song "Home Invasion" is that kids from all backgrounds are starting to think for themselves. They are starting to question their upbringings, their history lessons, and their religions. The Catholic and fundamentalist religions are pushed on kids so hard that they naturally rebel. White kids then say to their parents, "I'm into rock 'n' roll. I like Slayer." These kids aren't devil worshipers, as Tipper Gore in her PMRC newsletters would like you to believe. They are just rebelling against what their parents are trying to push on them. Their parents and the church immediately cry, "You'll go to the *devil*." After that, an even better way to flip on Mom is to say, "You know what? I like rap, too." That's what they call a double rebellion.

The church would have to come out of its lies for kids to start listening. The people who run the churches have to begin reading their book the way it's written. You could end racism before you could end religious arguments. There will always be holy wars, because religion is too handy a rallying tool for the people in power.

When America went to war in the Persian Gulf, it was so easy for our country's leaders to say, "Well, they're Muslims. They're fanatics." Or when they killed American Indians, they could say, "Well, they don't even believe in God. We can kill 'em. We can justify slaughtering them." So it's easy to get the American people to say, "Go get 'em! They're not even like us. They don't even believe in *God*, you know."

■ I tell you what we did: We stole your fucking kids.

Which is bullshit. I don't care who we slaughter. A hundred thousand dead equals a hundred thousand dead, murdered, end of story. Do you really think the lives of the Iraqis who died in the Persian Gulf War are less valuable than your own? Governments use religion as a tool to take the money and to take control and, more important, to keep you cheering their exploitation on and on.

Everybody wants to get in contact because everybody's trying to get to God. Everybody wants the power. The guy who says he knows God becomes, in effect, God. It's man's quest to be God. Or at least his best friend.

How a minister or a pope or a bishop has better contact than me, I simply don't know or understand. I'll *never* understand that. We're all born the same. The same question applies with royalty. Why is someone king or queen when you're not? Because they can be. Because you allow it.

As long as you allow these myths to be perpetuated, the church will never come out from behind its lies. Americans are clinging to their beliefs because this is how they hold on to their power. Zealots can read the book and angle it any convenient way they want. The scariest thing is, a lot of people really believe the trip they're on. They feel they're on a mission, and this is what they must do. Maybe this mission is a source of fulfillment for them, but more than likely, it's a substitute for something lacking in their own lives.

I think people need a lot more confidence rather than religion. Spirituality can be a crutch you rely on instead of handling your own business. Spirituality can help you, but it can also hinder you. People who send all their money to televangelists and just sit around waiting for the check to come in the mail need to know that check ain't never gonna come.

Spirituality is a good accessory to add to your life, but

■ **The home invader. This is a home invasion. Home invasion.**
■ **Home invasion.**

127

before anybody can get anything going right they have to have confidence in themselves. They have to believe they can and should do everything with or without God.

Once you can gain the momentum and walk your own walk, spirituality will come in behind you and give you a boost to help guide you in your own direction.

You alone have to decide the direction you want to go in. The spirit won't give you one. If you sit home and say, "Tell me. Give me a message. What should I do?" it won't. It'll say, "Make a move, and if you move in the right direction, I'll come right in there and give you that backup you're needing."

When I go through drama, I don't pray. There's something else that's pushing me and giving me power. I just think prayer shouldn't be relied on totally. Don't ever believe anything blindly. Always use your own head and your own heart to determine your beliefs. Don't even believe me without thinking it through.

After all, this is just my opinion on religion, who gives a fuck.

■ All right, we got the muthafuckin' kids, we outta here. C'mon.

128

Part III

YA SHOULDA KILLED ME LAST YEAR

7 Racism

A lot of y'all are probably racist. The quickest way to find out if you're racist is to ask yourself how you would feel if a black or Puerto Rican or Hispanic man went out with your sister.

Would that bother you?

If it does, then you're racist.

You really find out where you stand on this issue when intimacy is involved. You can say, "I don't mind black people. They're cool, they can hang around." But what if they fuck your sister or your daughter? What if they marry her and have children with her? Got a problem with that? You're racist.

Kids don't know what color they are, but they learn. Sooner or later somebody clues them in. When I lived in Summit, New Jersey, outside of Newark, I had this buddy, Mark. I didn't know he was white, I just knew he was my buddy. I used to play over at his house, and at night, Mark's

> If the white racists want to play this little game of supremacy, let's at least get the sides right.

mother would let all the other kids continue to play, but I was always sent home.

So I asked my mother, "How come Mark's mother makes me go home every night?" She said, "That's what it means to call people colored. You have to go home, because you're colored. I'm not gonna teach you about it now. But you'll learn about it. You'll learn."

In second grade, I became friends with this other white kid, Todd. Everybody played at Todd's house after school because he had all the cool toys. A buddy from my neighborhood, Kenneth, wanted to come play with us. Kenneth was a dark-skinned black kid, and Todd told him, "No, I can't have any more kids in my house." And I told Kenneth, "Cool, all right, Ken, I'm gonna go to Todd's house." And Ken said, "It's cool. I'll see you tomorrow." So we walked home and on the way about five more white kids rolled up and Todd said, "Come on over to my house." So I asked him, "I thought you couldn't have any more friends." And he said, "Oh, Kenneth's a darkie." Right then I realized Todd thought I was white.

That was my introduction to racism.

My mother was really light-skinned, lighter than me. Her side of the family was Creole—a mix of French and black. My father was dark. What or who I was, I really didn't know. My mom died when I was in third grade, and my dad passed when I was in seventh grade. I was kind of left alone to figure everything out. I'd grown up in a black neighborhood, so I didn't think too much about it.

In the military, I was called nigger this, nigger that, and I just learned to tolerate it. I really got a heavy dose of how deep racism runs on my first L.A. job, a gig for the Los Angeles Legal Aid Foundation. We used to process general denials, or evictions. I shared an office with a Mexican woman who

■ "Yo, Ice, you been down with the struggle for a long time, man.

talked like she was from the Valley. She was a lot savvier than me about racism. Every day, she'd say, "I'm telling you, these landlords are so racist. . . ." And I would nod, "Yeah, yeah, yeah," but I didn't really think much of it. She used to shake her head and say, "No, these people really are!"

We fielded phone calls from the landlords, and whenever she was on the phone, they assumed they were talking to a white girl. She would ask them why the tenants hadn't paid the rent, and the landlords would just ramble on to her. "Oh these fucking Mexicans, you know how they are. Lazy spicks." She would egg them on—"Is that right?" They kept right on talking. "Those chink motherfuckers, those niggers, blam, blam, blam. . . ." These fools not only thought they were talking to a white chick, they figured she would agree with them.

Wrong. We started taping the conversations and playing them for the Legal Aid attorneys—all of whom were Hispanic and black. They knew how to handle these people. They started using the tapes in court, and the jury ruled in favor of the tenant every time.

As you get older, racism doesn't go away. It just builds and builds and builds. At any given time, I might have more money in the bank than a middle-aged white lady will ever see in her life, but if I'm strolling through a mall in Chicago, she'll clutch her purse nervously when she sees me coming. People will eye me suspiciously in the stores. I see them sweat next to me on elevators. You just get used to it. It ain't no big thing. Black people are just used to that shit. You just expect that kind of reaction.

Other people will wonder how you can take it. But I figure I've got two options: I could just be pissed at the world twenty-four hours a day, every day, or I can just go on about my business and look at them like they're dumb. And I pick

■ **Why don't you drop some knowledge**

the second option, because that's just how this country is, and these people are programmed. Somewhere along the line, you just learn to tolerate it.

Some people don't tolerate it, and they learn to hate. I just never could get into that. I just looked at the stupid people like trapped animals. They are trapped in their own fears. I do get irritated, however, when someone says, "Oh, Ice T, it's not as bad as it used to be. You should go see what it's like down South." My whole attitude is, it all looks bad, you know? None of it's cool. It's just not cool.

My manager's name is Jorge Hinojosa—his father's Bolivian and his mother's white—and when I met him he was having his problems. Nobody was getting his name right, and he was tired of fighting it. He was ready to change his name to something else, and I told him, "Dude, you can't give it up, man. That's your name. That's who you are. Fuck these mutherfuckas if they don't like it. Let them learn how to spell it and pronounce it. If they don't dig you having that name and you want to change it so you fit in with their fucked-up rules, that's gonna be the biggest sale you ever did. That's your life." He stuck it out. But a lot of people make these concessions just so they can get along in the system, and it's just bullshit.

Sometimes I think of changing my last name to "X," because the only way you're going to know yourself is to first be in touch with yourself. That holds true for white people, too. I don't need any white people coming up to me and saying, "Yo, I'm black." Why don't you say, "Yo, I'm white, and I understand what's going on and I'd like to be down."

That's the most helpful tack you can take. A Crip will tell you, "No one can stop this war but us." It's the same thing with racism. Blacks don't want to leave the solution up to the white power structure, because we know it won't get handled. You can't just say, "White people got to do this,

■ For these brothers who want to get involved in this war."
■ Take notes, real gangsters wear trench coats.

134

white people got to do that," because you'd be falling back into letting the white man take care of you. So we have to make our move. A white person who wants to be down can really help by just not being a racist. That's what you can do. That's one less person who judges me because of my color.

I've taken the task upon myself of telling black people not to hate white people. Now, who has the harder task? The media are constantly perpetuating the fear—"Black black black black crime black crime black black black black black riots black black black . . ." So now you're gonna tell somebody who's white, "You shouldn't just hate black people." And they're staring at the tube: "Look on TV. Look what they do. Look what I see." When I tell a black guy to not hate whites, he'll start taking me back to B.C.: "They've been fucking us blind since day one. . . ."

As a consequence, you've got people on both sides of the fence who don't want to mix. "Aryans" try to maintain the power by spouting racist dogma. Muslims tell black men to stop looking outside their race for happiness. Consider this: If everybody was fucking everybody else, the world would have to change. If we had a mono-type race, everyone would have to get along. People have to start looking beyond color, regions, and neighborhoods and realize we're all from earth. If everybody bred cross-culturally, you wouldn't hate so much. I have no fear of everybody getting along. We all have one blood, we're all from the same God.

I had my baby boy with my girl, who's Hispanic. So, little Ice is Mexican and black. We had his first birthday party, and all the Mexican aunts and uncles were there and all my homies were there. Everybody was just kicking it, hanging out together celebrating my son's big day. Now, how you gonna hate in a situation like that? How can I not love my child? My friends and relatives can't get mad at anybody, because that little boy is my son.

■ Gray suits, black ties, and they seek votes.

So that's how you bring people together.

I asked Everlast, who raps with House of Pain, if he thought white people hate black people, or black people hate white people.

He told me he doesn't think black people hate white people; he just thinks they don't trust them. He doesn't think white people hate black people; he just figures they're afraid of them.

"If you were in a car accident, and I hit you, you would get out of your car a certain way because you were in the right," he told me. "And I'd get out of the car a little bit afraid. And the longer we live in the attitude that it's cool to oppress people, the longer we're going to be afraid. It'll only change once we say, 'Yo, this shit is wrong. Let's be equal.' "

He says a lot of people aren't willing to do that because they want to keep that edge up, the edge that they created for themselves throughout history. The white power structure didn't set up the game plan so black Americans would get equal wages and equal representation.

"Imagine going to the movies and everybody you see is black. And turn on TV, and everyone you see is black. And you go into a record company, and everybody is black. White people wouldn't stand for that. They'd go crazy if *they* didn't have equal rights."

Racism is programmed into people, I don't believe it's in-inherent. If you take three babies—a black kid, a white kid, an Asian kid—and you put them all in a sandbox and leave them alone, they'll all grow up and learn to love each other like a family until some asshole adult comes around and says, "You shouldn't like them—their skin is lighter." Or "Their skin is darker."

The bottom line is you have to determine whether or not you believe somebody can be evil from birth. That's what

■ And you're not to be misled.

makes the difference. I just don't believe that; I believe it's taught and it's driven into your brain. That's why there's so much fear of rap. Rap is saying, "Don't be afraid of me, all right? I'm mad, I'm pissed, but now I just don't look like a wild man in a cage. You know why I'm mad."

If you didn't know anything about black people you'd look at a riot and say, "Savages. Look at them. Look what they're doing to themselves."

Now you can look at it, and say, "This is wrong. Something's gotta change." That's what my *Home Invasion* album is all about. You've got kids now saying, "Wait a minute, Moms. The shit is fucked up. Cleopatra wasn't white like fucking Elizabeth Taylor, and we ain't built no pyramids. And there are thirty-six precious elements in the world, and 28 of them come out of fucking Africa. What's really going on? What really happened at the Alamo? What makes Asians the enemy? What is a Puerto Rican? What is a Jamaican? What made John Wayne such a great fucking man? He killed Indians! Aren't they Native Americans?"

All these questions are now being raised. We are entering a renaissance period, an educational revolution, where people are questioning the lies. People know shit's got to get right. Our country can't run off lies for much longer. The key to keeping the lies alive for the racists was the elimination of communication. They kept saying, "Don't let them communicate. Don't let them talk to each other. They'll never know how much they have in common." So when we came along with rap, we splashed this shit up. The kids reevaluated their knowledge. "What the fuck have I been learning?" started echoing around the country.

You can't accuse a lot of black kids of racism. We're dealing with a reaction, not an action. When we started believing that people are born evil, that was the beginning of racism. What you're really saying is there is no hope.

◀ **They'll kill you in your fucking bed.**

Once you can say there is no hope for black people, there's a reason to hate. They're ain't no hope. But as long as you believe people can change, there is hope. I think this country has a chance to grow out of its racist background. I'm just thinking of generations of kids and the way they think. The power base has to change.

White supremacists are struggling to hold on to their power. These aren't just a bunch of guys running around in sheets. Racism runs deep in the heart of so many Americans. That's why a lot of people don't like to see interracial marriages or even admit they exist. Any child with pigmentation is considered black. So if your mama's white and your dad's black, you're black. Racists are terrified we're all gonna get together because if we do, we can systematically eliminate the white race. That's what Public Enemy's *Fear of a Black Planet* is all about. The white race is the only race that requires two white people to make a white baby. Whoever made up the rules felt they had to be pure, and they had to remain pure. White supremacists fucked themselves on that kind of thinking, because around the year 2010, they're gonna definitely be headed toward minority status. It's an Aryan Nation nightmare, a catch-22. They are fucked now, because if people just get along, you can eliminate the white race.

Now, somebody who isn't racist wouldn't give a fuck. In your heart, your baby will just be beautiful, not black or white. But to racists, that black or semi-black baby may as well be dead. Any black person who is not pitch-black has white blood in them. I don't know where mine comes from, and I don't care. Aryan people are terrified, though. They know they have to keep perpetuating the fear between races. They are definitely on a move to kill up some shit before it goes on.

If you don't believe me, remember there are white people who *really* believe they are superior. You just got to remember that. And that attitude originates from them believing they are the son of God, and therefore, they are superior. Once you understand that, it's less difficult to see the conspiracies of everything around us and how they create the negatives and positives, i.e. devil's-food cake (black) vs. angel-food cake (white). Black is the color of death and evil. White is the color of goodness and light. In America, the correct color to be is white. We're "colored people." Why aren't white people called "people without color"? The danger is it all becomes twisted in with your self-worth and the value you put on your own head. When you come to these realizations, nothing really changes. When it gets down to it, you're just sitting up there going along with it, going along with a system that doesn't work.

Sometimes it amazes me that the black race is still in existence. So many tricks were played on my people throughout history. Babies were snatched from their families and deprived of their ancestral and cultural history. When that happens, how the fuck do you know who you are? Under those circumstances, how can you expect people to start off some three hundred years later and catch up with you? You are presenting them with an impossible task. So, whenever you hear, "Black people are ignorant, they're dumb, they can't talk," you have to remember that white society only allowed them into the game a few years back. They are for all practical purposes still struggling to get in. In that respect, we're fucking incredible. Even the true racists know black people aren't dumb; they know we've only been riding in the front of the bus for only the past thirty years. They also know that with access to the same opportunities, we will excel.

Throughout American history, the culture of black people has been marketed, exploited, and even stolen. When I worked for Warner Brothers, the fact I was "street" became a marketing angle. A friend told me that Eddie Murphy once

■ But they don't look that much like me or you.

said, "I get paid to hold my dick." And when you really break it down, he *is* getting paid to hold his dick on cue. "Okay, roll it. Be black. Be street muthafucka. But do it when I say so."

Even if Murphy's not happy about it, the flip side is he's making money he can then reinvest in his friends and family, and that's what makes someone happy. Since I've made a few dollars, I've been able to get my buddies out of jail. I've been able to take my buddies' parents to hospitals they couldn't have gotten into before, and I've taken guys on tour for a year who would have stayed home and probably gotten shot otherwise.

Money allows you to help people. I don't want to hear about how noble it is to be broke. You got a better shot if you got a few dollars in your pocket. You got a chance. You can survive out here. It's like that line in the film *Barfly*: "Nobody suffers like the poor."

Unfortunately, the actor who said that line in the film, Mickey Rourke, turns around in real life and says, "The reason for the riots are the movies like *Boyz N the Hood*." And I used to like Mickey Rourke. I thought to myself, why would he have to say some stupid shit like that?

That's the scary thing about racism. Shit just comes out every once in a while. It just comes out. I've been guilty of racist remarks, and I'm learning and I'm reaching. When I did say something stupid, I was just using slang words. That's why I don't get angry if somebody says "nigger" or "spick" or whatever. Everybody throws these names around. Those words don't necessarily mean anything. I'm not saying if you throw a name at somebody to their face they are not going to hold that against you for the rest of their life. But sometimes people throw words around, and it's just a word. They didn't really mean any harm. If I say, "I hate you," you have to determine if I'm just momentarily angry or if I'm really prac-

■ But if you pull up the sheets and expose them,

ticing hate. People who hate somebody from their heart are a different story. There are people who really practice hating others. Those are the people you really recognize as dangerous, and you should be afraid of them.

If Axl Rose says "nigger" on a record, does that make him a racist? If Cube raps about putting a bullet in N.W.A. manager Jerry Heller's temple, does that make him anti-Semitic? You just don't know until you have an opportunity to meet people personally and then decide.

Before I met Axl, everybody just assumed I would hate him. I would tell them, "No, I ain't never met Axl Rose." When I did finally meet Axl Rose, he was the coolest dude. He's totally cool with me. When we were on tour in San Diego, Axl told me he's a victim of the press the same way I am. He asked me directly, "How many people do you think know me, man? I mean know me, kick it with me? There's nobody. Everybody's right and everybody says all this stuff about me because they are making money talking about Axl Rose. The promoters didn't want Body Count to come out here on this tour. I wanted Body Count to come out on tour."

That's the bottom line for me: He was cool with me. I'm here to say Axl Rose is a cool dude, but he's another victim of all the hype and the press. He asked me, "How am I supposed to be racist if Slash is black?" Slash is black whether people know it or not. Axl added, "Come again with that. Is there anything else they can throw at me? Do I beat my girl? I make records, man."

The press loves to take people down, though. Who knows, members of Guns N' Roses might do a little dope. I don't know; I never saw them do any. But as far as *guys* go, I don't see anything wrong with them.

The lead singer of Metallica, James Hetfield, the dude *Rolling Stone* called the "Leader of the Real Free World," that dude is a different story. He put out a real ill vibe to all

■ **They'll crawl up like snakes and show fangs of venom.**

my guys when we toured with Guns N' Roses and Metallica. Yeah, homeboy right there, he has a trip. Kirk Hammett, the lead guitar player, and Lars Ulrich, the drummer, are totally cool. Whenever you assess people, you have to judge each man for himself and not believe the hype or the press. If you don't, you are just starting the whole cycle all over again.

The whole problem with race relations is based around a lot of lies and a lot of ignorance. If you listen to members of the Aryan Nation talk, which I recommend for anybody who's trying to understand racism, it's all based on fear. "We're gonna be extinct. We're gonna be gone. We have to do something before them Negroes take over. We are the superior race." The scary thing is they talk this shit all in the name of God, which proves you can take any scripture and flip it to your favor if you want to.

When you read the Bible, which is supposedly the word of God, remember: God didn't write it. Man wrote it, and then the church deciphers it for you. People who follow the "word of God" should be very leery of who they're paying to do the interpretation for them.

I really don't fear these racists because the youth in the '90s are fighting in the other direction. I really think now, more than ever, the younger people are coming off that racist shit, and the movement is being spearheaded by music. I think Lollapalooza has great potential. Artists like Perry Farrell deserve a lot of credit because they have vision and they also have power. The white musicians are the artists up on the hill, and when they turn around and give credit to other cultures, people listen up. Lars Ulrich wrote in *Rolling Stone* that Body Count was his favorite metal band. He's giving us props. Throughout this whole struggle, that's all people are asking for. They just want some props, some respect. That's

■ Now I've been a soldier for years,
■ Representing the tattooed tears.

142

why Marky Mark isn't hated. When somebody like Marky comes out and raps, all we say is, "Well, rap, man. . . . Prove to us you can rap." That's the same way white kids were with me and rock. White kids looked at Body Count and said, "Okay, we're not gonna judge you guys, but don't pose, Ice. Give us some real rock." People accept it if it's real. Michael Bolton wins best R & B artist because it's not a matter of color to a lot of people. It's a matter of if you accomplish what you say you're going to accomplish, and Bolton sings his fucking heart out.

Vanilla Ice ran into problems because he lied, not because he was white. Instead of coming out and saying, "Hey, I'm a white kid out of Texas, and I'm trying to rap," he came out with a hardcore pose: "I'm from the street and I'm down." When you say you're from the street, that carries a lot of weight. A lot of black people can't say they're from the street. From the street means you might have been on dope, you might have been homeless. You earned your money on the street without any outside job or parents for help. You hustled on the streets of Harlem. Somehow you came up with something to sell so you could make it to another day. You *lived* and *worked* the street. You had a buck forty for dinner and there was no goddamn food. You were out there scrambling. Unfortunately, there are too many kids who are from that street, but Vanilla Ice ain't one.

I used to ask about Vanilla Ice, "What street is he from, Sesame Street?" People in rap have the Elvis fear: Watching something they created get taken away from them again. I've read some magazines that declare Marky Mark the king of hip-hop. That upsets a lot of people. Even though *he's* not propagating it, it still hurts people.

They don't hate Marky Mark for it. He's a whole 'nother kind of kid. He's Donny Wahlberg's brother, and Donny is

■ **Other brothers locked up with no choice.**
■ **Left in the bowels of the devil with no voice.**

like a black/white kid. Not a '92 Turnout—somebody who latched on when it became trendy to be down. He really grew up around black people and is deep in the culture.

It's really where you've grown up. The color of your skin isn't what gives you the flavor, the juice and the angle of seeing things. It's who you are and how you're livin'. It's the people you're around. If a white baby grows up in Nickerson Gardens, an L.A. housing project, he will talk like me, he will walk like me, and he might even be the craziest little gangbanger you've ever seen.

If you take a black child and put him in a Simi Valley home and keep him there—don't let him associate with kids in the 'hood—he will grow up to be like Bryant Gumbel. To me, Gumbel is the epitome of a black-skinned white person— his speech, his talk and how he carries himself. For all I know, Bryant Gumbel might be a *cool* motherfucker, but on TV, he portrays a dude who gave up all his black culture to get a job. He strikes me as the kind of black guy who would call gangbangers niggers, and use the word in its most negative sense.

Maybe he's another product of his environment. Like the Black Panthers used to say, if you think the system works for you and you agree with it, you're in the white. If the system is against you and you're questioning authority, you're in the black.

The enemy is the person who judges straight off skin color. You have to know who they are in order to fight it. The fucked-up thing that people in the black know is, no matter what you do, you'll always be a nigger. So, Bryant, listen up: You're a nigger, man.

Anybody trying to get into the white is just being foolish. There's no way around that. I'm proud to be a nigger. I know I'm in the majority. Not only are blacks niggers, but Indians are niggers, Jews are niggers, Koreans are niggers, Hispanics

■ **My phones are tapped, my crib is bugged.**

144

are niggers, Puerto Ricans are niggers, WASPs who like black people are niggers. If the white racists want to play this little game of supremacy, let's at least get the sides right. If you want to play this game of racism, let's not just be the blacks here on one side, let's all unify. Then let's see if they want to continue to play.

I'm very glad the Koreans and blacks are starting to get together down in South Central. The Hispanics in Los Angeles are also striving toward unity, and it's this type of energy that can finally make South Central a community. If this kind of cooperation continues, it's really going to be a different game soon. That's what's going down right now in the '90s.

Currently, this is one of my main focuses. As I go around and lecture to campuses and talk to different kids on tour, I'm eager to spread this message of unity. They want to know what's going on and want to know what the first step is. I'm very excited right now, because I'm reaching the kids. It's a matter of what they've been taught, and I'm gonna do my best to keep un-teaching.

Right now, people are reaching out for each other. White kids are reaching for black culture. People are reaching out for understanding of each other, but it's gonna take time. A lot of white kids tell me, "Yo, Ice, I want to be down. But black people, you know, they ain't receptive." I try to explain to them: "Look, man, shit has been fucked up for four hundred years, right? It's gonna take a while, it might take a hundred and fifty years before it changes. You can't be like, 'You should accept me because I'm wearing this Malcolm X T-shirt.' You know, you gotta be patient, you gotta show love." It may take another two hundred years to undo past damage. We can instill love into our kids, but we're gonna have to push and push and push before we see any of this shit change.

I sometimes wish for quick fixes, too. I want to tell these

◀ **My car is tailed from club to club.**

kids, "Okay, I'm black. Don't listen to your parents, and what have I done to you? Nothing." There you go, I've eliminated racism. But unfortunately, it's not that simple. It's going to be hard to mend. But I know it can mend, and this generation has to start the mending.

Whenever I hear people saying they are trying and their efforts aren't being well received, I tell them they aren't trying hard enough. If there's a pro-choice or a pro-life rally, white people will be out in the streets adamantly protesting and sitting in and crashing the line. But have a civil rights or racial issue, and y'all don't come out.

Every race has to show and prove. Black and white people have to work harder to set things right. I personally judge a devil by his deeds, not by his color. I'm checking everybody out. Since I know a white kid has been more programmed to hate me, I'm checking him out maybe twice. But the brothers, I'm checking them out too, dig? 'Cause more brothers have killed my brothers than anybody white since I've been alive. So everybody's got to show and prove.

When I look to the future, I see a day far away—but I see it—where we can get up and get it together if we don't blow this whole shit up sooner.

However, that's just my opinion on racism, who gives a fuck.

■ **And this ain't no fucking joke.**

8
Riots and Revolution

April 29, 1992, was the happiest day of my entire life. I'm so proud the people got out there and made some muthafuckin' noise when the four LAPD officers who beat on Rodney King were found innocent in Simi Valley. Anybody who says this uprising was ignorant is the stupidest muthafucka in the world. Rage ignites the fire but once the flames get going, poverty takes over. The bottom line was people were broke.

The press was quick to report, "Well, they're just looting."

Yeah, because they're fuckin' broke. They look at big stores, like the Good Guys, as being the system, and the system owes 'em. They're saying, "Pay, muthafucka."

The media also gives you a front-row seat to the riot scene, showing only the effect of anguish but not the cause. They'll take you to the stoops

> The absence of noise is not the presence of peace.
> —The Reverend Jesse Jackson
> April 17, 1993

■ They want to see a nigger broke.

147

of the Imperial Gardens housing project, but they don't take you inside. They don't show you how people are living in there. How are these brothers living? Why are people so goddamn angry? Why did they take you only to the 'hood? A lot of the people looting in the '92 riots were white. The majority of the looters were Hispanic.

If they'd done that, maybe some of you who didn't participate would've gotten up off your ass to do something about it. If you were living that broke, and you had watched your people get beaten, you wouldn't just sit around and wait on justice. Fuck that. You wouldn't let anybody hold a badge over your head, no cross, nothin', and beat you down. Fuck that.

You don't get any of *that* from television; they only show the reaction to people's humiliation. Throughout Rodney King's federal trial, where the jury found two of the four officers accused of beating him guilty, the media focused all week on the mobilization of the police force—the mobilization that we paid $1.5 million a day for. Add $1.5 million a day to the $58,600,000 L.A. taxpayers paid from April 1983 to April 1992 in police-brutality settlements and judgments. Who were the police really protecting you from? They were protecting you from having to look directly in the face of how bad people are living, and how tired they are of being beaten down by cops and society.

The scary part of the uprising was not that Rodney King got beaten—they've been whipping our ass for years—and not that the white cops did it, but that the jury, the first twelve in a box, found the cops innocent. How many of our brothers are in prison right now because the current jury system found them guilty? The system is flawed at best. What are your options when there is no videotape? After you lose a fucked-up trial what's next? Playing two out of three? That's called an appeal, and that's a luxury of the rich.

■ **You can't slip, if you slip you're out.**

148

When the riots jumped off they immediately rushed up to me and put me on Channel 11. The newscaster said to me: "Ice, stop the riots." Stop the riots? Who the fuck am I? One thing I make sure not to do is believe for a second anybody thinks I'm something special. I told him, "Whoever could have stopped it could have prevented it." Nobody stepped in and prevented it.

They started rolling the tape, and I said: "You know, I hate to tell you I told you this was gonna happen, but it hurts me to see my neighborhood going up like this 'cause that's where I grew up. At the same time, I can't honestly say that if I didn't have this money in my pocket, and I wasn't who I was, that I wouldn't be there, too."

The producers then started yelling, "Get him off. Get him off the TV."

I was going down. I had to speak from my heart, though. If I'd been in control of the riots, I would've moved on the police, and I would've been locked up like Geronimo Pratt. "Stop the riots"—yeah, right.

When you deal with people from the ghetto, remember every other person's got somebody in jail, somebody they know who's locked up. When people saw that verdict in Simi Valley, it not only meant the cops got off, but also people said to themselves, "Yo, my boy's in jail, and I'm watching these muthafuckas go free. What about my daddy?"

That's completely different from the typical white attitude: "Oh, that's a travesty of justice." Most minorities have got somebody in their lives who's served. The acquittal hit the two classes completely differently.

People from the ghetto lashed out. They aimed at Korean people because they felt Koreans were one step above them, so that's the closest step to the system. They didn't know the Koreans are just as broke as them. The best thing that resulted

■ You gotta know what you're talking about.

149

from that mix is there now is communication between the Koreans and the blacks in the community. Communication is now at an all-time high.

Before this could all go down, however, people had to fight. Once the smoke cleared, they sat down and held discussions in an attempt to solve their differences. Koreans are now moving back into the community, but it's a little bit different. It boils down to this: They've got the store—the Korean banks offer excellent loan opportunities to their own immigrants when they first arrive in this country—but your little brother might have been coming here for months trying to get a job.

The black community wanted to know why they wouldn't hire their kids. Prior to the discussions, the Koreans' philosophy was to hire only within their own community. An attitude like that isn't necessarily wrong, but it's not what the community needed. Once you take a job out of the inner city, where does the black kid go? He ain't got no place to go. So when the people struck out, they struck out at what they thought was the power—the people who most directly oppressed them.

The riots opened a dialogue. If you walk into any Korean-owned liquor store in South Central Los Angeles now, you'll see a young sister or a young brother working there, which is only right. So it's going down. People in the community need to support each other as much as possible. Everybody within South Central needs to work together. Sometimes you have to fight with your brothers in order to really be brothers.

The death toll between the two groups was kept down, thankfully. Did you ever wonder why you never heard much about the fifty-seven people who died? Because most of them were shot by cops. That's why it's so difficult for me to understand how the community could be won over by the

■ Drop science every chance you get
■ Hit direct and indirect

150

LAPD's show of force before the federal trial. These cops were presenting a challenge to people in the community, when all the people really wanted was justice. They don't want to go head up with the National Guard. They want some justice.

Muthafuckas are so ignorant to say that people wanted a riot, an excuse to loot. Bullshit. If they wanted to riot, why didn't they riot when they saw the videotape? Because they waited on justice. They said, "Okay. The tape is here. We got 'em. Put 'em in jail. Let's move on." And when it didn't happen the first time around, the shit hit the fan and people issued their own consequence.

In the words of Eldridge Cleaver, from *Soul on Ice:* "If we do not get our manhood, this earth will be leveled." That's all we want. People just want to be treated equally or they will kill somebody.

The most peaceful time I ever experienced in South Central was during the riots. While everybody was looking for fires, we walked through the streets. Kids were setting shit on fire, people were smiling. Everybody was shaking each other's hands, feeling a camaraderie. It was as if the people had taken the city back. For those few days, it belonged to us and it was peaceful.

It was like the eye of the hurricane, chaos swirled around you but you were there, and it was so calm inside. Everybody on the outside said, "Oh, it's terrible down in there." But if you were one of the people inside South Central, it was beautiful. I was rolling through the neighborhood signing autographs.

When I drove back into Hollywood, I ran into members of Queer Nation, and they were fucking shit up. I started rolling with the Nation while they were yelling, "Fuck the police." It was the wildest shit in the world.

What you saw on TV was not what it was. There were

█ Speak in code 'cause you're never alone.
█ That's why I use this low tone.

white people downtown at Parker Center tearing shit up, too. There were even a lot of white people in the middle of South Central protesting and trying to help in any way they could. They were taken right into the community. There were no stories about that.

The media took that one incident at the corner of Florence and Normandie, where four homeboys beat one truck driver, Reginald Denny, and twisted it into the defining moment of the riots. "Okay, our job's done. This is what the riots were about." Right after the incident, I was questioned about the beating, and I told reporters that as far as I was concerned, the L.A. Four were just impersonating officers.

I'm gonna tell you something a lot of people do not understand: The guys who pulled Denny out of the truck would've pulled a black dude out of that truck. Their actions were motivated by anger, not racism. He was there, they were mad, he got snatched up out of that truck, and it was on.

You don't hear about the four black people who rescued Denny and drove him to a hospital. You don't hear anything about the black doctor who operated on him. L.A. is not this one-dimensional place. Even Denny now goes on television and speaks eloquently on society's need to explore where the rage comes from. He is attempting to understand.

At the same time Denny was getting beaten, black people were getting their cars blown up and were being snatched out of their cars—it was madness right there. The Denny incident was not about race.

In any type of war situation, or in a riot, everybody down there ain't stable. A lot of people are crazy, gung-ho. People were taking shots at firemen. Why? I don't know. I talked to some brothers who said they probably saw the uniform and thought they were police. People were tripping. There was nothing simple about the reasons that people did what they did.

■ **Follow this and you might grow older.**

152

If the four officers who beat King had all gotten off on round two, the federal trial, there would've been some dead mutha-fuckin' pigs and some dead kids in the street. I just hope Officers Laurence Powell and Stacey Koon get stretched, be-cause I fear if we have another uprising, people will get really hurt this time. What you saw last time was a tantrum. When a prisoner rebels, he lights his own mattress on fire. He lashes out at the objects around him. People stupidly criticized this the first time around: "Why would they tear up their own neighborhoods?" You don't want people to go out with guns and start shooting people, do you? Then you got real chaos. The National Guard would come in and start killing people and you'd have a full-scale war. With all the guns on the street right now, the U.S. government wouldn't think twice about napalming the whole area.

The 'hood doesn't want to go head up with the govern-ment. That's not what it is. People only want to see things set right. The riot said, "I don't really want to go out and hurt you, can't you see this? Look over here, them mutha-fuckas are mad. They can't keep telling you they're mad, they're showing you some anger, some violence."

It's in your best interest to pay attention.

If people don't pay attention, though, shit's gonna get worse. The day before the federal trial's verdict was an-nounced, the city was working itself into frenzy over the possibility of violence: "There are so many guns on the street, and not enough cops on the force." As a guest on *Channel 4 News*, Jesse Jackson made this point: "The absence of noise is not the presence of peace."

Noise, by the American military's definition, has always entitled them to the use of guns. Why should it be different for people in the 'hood? Our government maintains you have the right to bear arms, because it's your last form of defense

■ **This is a message to the soldiers.**

against tyranny. Then politicians reason that we don't need automatic weapons, because you can't hunt with them. Who do people in the ghetto need to protect themselves from? Bears? No. The police, the only force that has directly fucked us over. To fight the tyranny of law enforcement, I don't need a hunting rifle, I need a Mac-10.

The right to bear arms is to protect yourself during revolution—or, to us, when the man turns into the enemy. If you could have seen the buildup of police officers the day before that second verdict dropped and not noticed that the city was drawing sides, then you were crazy. The city's approach to potential civil unrest was to stick guns under the noses of every brother in the ghetto. This time, there was no show of force, but what about next time?

Do not believe for a second that America is so intellectual that we are beyond revolution. It happened in Afghanistan, it could happen anywhere. Revolution doesn't necessarily mean the people would've won, but there would have been a lot of blood in the streets.

Whenever you as a citizen mess up, the system can issue a consequence. If you speed, consequence. If you steal, consequence. How do people issue a consequence on the system? Vote? No. We have the ability to issue a consequence. What you saw on April 29, 1992, in Los Angeles was a consequence to the system's fuckup.

If consequences aren't issued, nothing changes. As long as a child keeps reaching up on the table and you do not issue a consequence, he will keep reaching up on that table. Can anybody tell me the consequence that should be issued to the government, beyond voting? No. There is none. You have to protest. You have to step to 'em.

If there is another uprising, stay in your bomb shelters with your canned food and arm yourself, 'cause it's gonna be a little late to be running up next to me wearing a Public

■ **Message to the soldiers.** ■ **Message to the soldiers.**

Enemy T-shirt and talking about equality. This is what they will call Judgment Day. People are going to be judged. And there are mostly gonna be black people out there because at this point, they are the angriest.

If you don't have a bomb shelter, stay home. And if you want to be really helpful to the cause, shoot the first muthafucka who ever taught you to hate.

I've spoken to Jello Biafra on these issues. I'm not talking about Jello pudding, Jello's deep, man. He used to front the Dead Kennedys, and he pointed out that every time you come up with a problem—and a lot of people are good at finding problems—spend the day trying to figure out how to fix it.

Take a moment to look beyond the rhetoric of the riots. Look beyond Rodney King and beyond the four officers. Look beyond Reginald Denny and the L.A. Four. Don't even bother looking at Daryl Gates. Okay, what do you have? What is the real crisis?

The crisis and the injustice in the inner city result from the lack of hope.

Now, how do you fix a lack of hope?

You create real opportunity. You don't just talk about it, you move on it. I want to see an educational revolution in this country that rivals anything that's ever taken place on this earth. Kids in America should be able to go to any school they want. If you want to pursue a Ph.D., you should be able to just continue going to school to do that for free.

I would never have gotten into crime if I had a decent education that had geared me toward a job. First off, we need to start running high schools more like colleges, to help prepare kids for real jobs. Early in their high school career, kids should be required to pick a major and work toward it. The teachers should ask them, "What would be your dream vocation?" Once you really answered that question, you could

■ Message to the soldiers. ■ Message to the soldiers.

start working toward that career. The whole system has to be revamped, so a kid wanting to be a doctor has more options than just a biology class. He can learn finance and sociology, too. This way, his dream won't be shattered when he gets out of high school. He will already be working toward a goal. Kids need to have direction much earlier in the game.

Kids shouldn't wait till graduation to determine what they want to be. Too many kids graduate with no clue of how to do anything but work in a minimum-wage job. Once a ghetto kid turns eighteen, he's pretty much cut off from money. Mama says, "Well, I've taken care of you up till now; now you go do something." The *last* reason you can't get an education should be money.

You should be able to further your education after high school with or without money. The statement that there are more black men in prison than in college should frighten this country into changing what's staring them in the face. Don't just build more prisons and hire more police officers, start paying teachers Gs; revamp our education system. It's a tragedy police officers make more than teachers. Teachers should be the highest-paid professionals in the country. Without teachers we got nothing.

How do you pay for this revolution? I can come up with $3 billion real quick to help out. Take one billion from the space program. That means we won't get a space station built in 2001. It will be completed in 2003. And it'll probably just mean one less water fountain or toilet seat.

Take another billion from the defense program. Take one Stealth bomber. We ain't using the Stealth bombers; the muthafuckas don't work. Ain't nobody gonna miss it. It's gonna be a real serious war when we need four fuckin' Stealth bombers. By then it won't matter anyway.

The last billion dollars should be snatched from law

■ Now they killed King and they shot X.
■ Now they want me, you could be next.

enforcement, because if people were in school there would be less crime.

That's three billion I just came up with, and I'm a fool right off the street. If that's still not enough money, then take these mega-industries called prisons and shut them down, because they won't be necessary. When is the last time you heard of a guy dropping out of law school and robbing a 7-11? When's the last time you heard of a guy who was studying to be a doctor stealing a car? That doesn't happen when you think you have a chance to do something else with your life. You're too busy working your brain toward a higher education. It's when your brain lies dormant and you're hanging on the corner, drinking and thinking of other ways to get over, that shit goes wack. Some people are ignorant enough to believe drinking's the problem. One lady stepped to me recently and said, "Malt liquor's the problem, Ice T. That's where it all starts."

I said, "Look, woman, I'm less concerned with the liquor. Let's get to the point of what makes a brother want to hang around and drink all day. What makes him think there's nothing else to do but just hold a 40 and cool out? That means he lost hope."

If you're studying for your Ph.D., you can hold that St. Ides. You can drink the hell out of that St. Ides for all I care. It's not the liquor. It's hanging out and not doing anything along with drinking. This is Jello Biafra's law of problem-solving: You've got to try to get to the bottom of the problems.

Now, I'm no politician, but why can't they come up with the money and the vision to fund an educational revolution? We came up with millions of dollars every day to watch Waco, Texas, burn. Why can't we come up with money to feed the minds of our children?

■ All you gotta do is speak too loud.
■ All you gotta do is be too proud.

Look at the current environment of inner-city schools. In junior high, you already have intense prison environments. You've got all these people pushing up against each other. Everybody's flexing, and kids are getting shot. This is what happens in schools when conditions deteriorate. They are overcrowded and teachers are underpaid; the whole system is fucked up. We need to build additional schools for these kids. My high school was nicknamed Fort Crenshaw. That environment is no way to inspire young minds.

The schools are so crowded that kids are being bused into the suburbs, and the gang problem is starting up all over again in white neighborhoods. This whole violent cycle begins from a lack of money being pumped into the youth facilities early on. The well-being and the education of kids have to be our top priorities just for this country to survive.

America has such great potential. Quality education should be something that's provided for our people. It will eventually fix our lopsided economy. Look at the Japanese economy. We dropped a few bombs on them, right? Their government came back and said, "Okay, cool, trip off this. We don't even have an army no more, we'll just put our money into education and buy the United States."

I know if our country put its collective mind to work, we could have this revolution intellectually and intelligently, because I don't want to do this violently.

I've got the plan, but I'm not running this shit yet. We have to look at who is running the country to see if there is any hope. People voted for change this year, and we now have a Democrat in the White House. Is this new president gonna implement change for us? Historically, the chances are bleak. None of them have really affected dramatic change in the past.

I don't like Clinton personally, because he reminds me of a used-care salesman. I'm a con artist and I've seen a

■ 'Cause once you let 'em know who you are and where you're at

smooth con, and this muthafucka's got a smooth con. Plus, if he got Hillary to believe that story about Gennifer Flowers, we know he's good. He's one slick cat. Even if Clinton came correct, he's got to first begin undoing the damage twelve years of Reagan Republicans inflicted on the country.

I'm gonna explain to you who Bush is, for those of you who are still curious about the man. I'm going to use my "Asshole Factor" tally, which you might find to be a handy tool in the future.

You know that cop who pulls you over, who didn't really have to give you a ticket but he gave it to you anyway? We're gonna multiply him 100 times, and now you have the chief of police. Multiply him about 100 times, and you've got an FBI agent. Multiply the agent approximately 1,000 times and you've got the head of the FBI. Multiply him 10,000 times and you've got a CIA agent. Multiply this agent another 10,000, and you've got the head of the CIA.

Bush was the head of the CIA. Bush has to be an asshole the size of a fuckin' black hole. I have information for you: You don't get to be the head of the CIA by being a hell of a nice guy. Read anything you want on the CIA—covert action, assassination, overthrowing governments—and see what I'm talking about. (I also recommend the *The Conspirator's Hierarchy: The Committee of 300*.) This muthafucka could probably put his hand on a polygraph test and blow the machine up. He's as close as you can come to the Antichrist as possible.

For all we know, Bush is dead and there's been a guy with a *Mission Impossible* mask walking around posing as him for the last four years. That's what the CIA is about. So how do you trust Bush? Read my lips. We know he's the best liar in the world.

I really wanted to vote in this last presidential election, but my motto was, "If God had wanted us to vote he'd have

■ **You better watch your back.**

159

given us candidates." Or at the very least, the ballot could have offered a "None of the Above" category.

I'm praying to God Clinton makes a fool out of me and does the right thing. He got in there and attempted to make some radical moves right out front, but the political process leaves me cold for the most part. What does a president really do other than shake hands? He's got other people working for him. He's an icon. He's primarily in the White House so it looks like we've got someone in control.

It's really up to the people to make some noise and stir this shit up. L.A.'s tantrum brought the focus of the world to South Central for a brief moment in time, and for that brief moment, the rest of the world had a conscience. I fear that since then the city has already gone back to business as usual. As long as you lie dormant and take it, they will continue to fuck you over.

Even though I'm pushing all my positive hopes and dreams forward, be prepared for the other side—the violent side, you know what I'm saying? I'm prepared; how about you?

That's my opinion on riots and revolution, who gives a fuck.

■ 'Cause you might think you're just dope,

9 The Controversy

To understand "The Controversy," you must first understand that free speech does not really exist in America. If I believed in free speech, I'd be crazy by now. I'd be sitting up here like a lunatic whimpering over my First Amendment rights.

The Constitution is just a figment of all our imaginations. There is no Bill of Rights. There are no Amendments. They simply do not exist.

Think about it for a moment: Two hundred years ago, when the Constitution was written, I was considered property. Now the mind-set of anybody who can draft a constitution is to say, "Everything looks okay, doesn't it? This is as right as we can get it. Uh-huh, black people are slaves. White people own everything and have all the power. Any questions?"

They were *insane*. How could you believe you could own somebody

Warner Brothers cannot afford to be in the business of black rage.

■ **While you're living in a sniper's scope.**

and sense you were doing something right? The entire Constitution is void. It was written by lunatics.

Throughout the controversy, people defended me on the grounds of the First Amendment. "Oh, Ice T has the right to say this under the First Amendment." Fuck the First Amendment. I have the right under *God* to say anything I want to say from my heart that comes out of my mouth. I do not need a law to say what I can or cannot say. I am a human being, put on this earth, and I can say any muthafuckin' thing I want.

As soon as you make a law to tell you what you can say, the same law will tell you what you can't say, you see? Fuck the muthafuckin' First Amendment.

I've been surrounded by controversy since I started making records. Any time you ever say something the conservative masses disagree with, you've made a controversial statement. If you were to say, "Kill all the pigeons," and everybody in the world hated pigeons, that wouldn't be a controversial statement.

The power brokers in this country rarely agree with anything I have to say. The reason is simple: I am a black man, and my agenda is counter to their agenda. Their agenda is to maintain the status quo. My agenda is to flip the status quo and allow the people on the bottom to get to the top. Naturally, the people on the top want to stay there, but it's my aim to see that everybody can get to the top.

Capitalist systems don't operate like that. They require an upper, middle, and lower class. But I don't give a fuck about that kind of system. I want to change it. So everything that comes out of my mouth—my ideals, my attitude—will conflict with their beliefs.

One reason I'm regarded as being so controversial is I say exactly what's on my mind. There is little question that people know when they're about to jump off and give the

■ I'm not trying to scare you, but there's danger if you get too deep.

masses a taste of an ugly truth. They know the masses will disagree with them and deny the statement.

The real question is: How many people will actually come out and speak the truth?

A lot of artists, actors, and businesspeople agree with a lot of the shit I say, but they're just too scared to say it themselves. If they express themselves, they might lose their jobs or their status.

People are always telling me, "Don't say that. Don't say that." I just continue to speak. Every other statement I make in this book won't ever get me a Nike commercial or a Coke commercial, because in order to get big sponsorships from these companies, you have to buy into the American way. You have to say, "The president is great. There is no racism. Let's pay our taxes. Isn't this country great? Red, white, and blue. The Persian Gulf War, yeah!"

Everybody sing along: "We are Americans. We are Americans."

When you join that club, you win all the prizes.

As much as I would like to do a Nike commercial with Michael Jordan, it's not important enough to me that I would change my beliefs. I really have no options because my way of thinking is not the norm for the American way, which is the mind-set of the people who really run everything. The power brokers perpetuate this American myth, and it's the sanctity of this myth they protect—even if they have to kill in the name of protecting the myth itself.

Long before "Cop Killer" was released and my career would be publicly defined by a four-minute sound bite, I was dealing with the enemy. I've been going through these shitstorms since '87, when I dropped *Rhyme Pays*. It was the first album ever stickered, and I was the first real rapper to come out and use a lot of profanities and talk crazy.

■ **Some nights I don't sleep.**

When I dropped *Power* in 1988, people went after the album's cover, which, you'll recall, had the infamous photograph of my girlfriend in a bikini holding a gun. They also came after the song "I'm Your Pusher," which is an anti-drug song. Without even knowing what the song was about, people flipped. "Are you saying you're selling dope, Ice T?"

When I went to speak at junior high schools, the FBI called Warner Brothers and said: "We don't think Ice T is the appropriate person to speak at schools."

"Why not?"

"Because of the album cover."

"He doesn't intend to distribute the album while lecturing at the schools."

"Well, what about this record, 'I'm Your Pusher?' Do you think that's right for the kids?"

"Have you heard the record?"

"No. We don't have a phonograph at the Bureau."

The FBI condemned just on sight, without thinking or listening. "Pusher" is an anti-drug song. This is the type of ignorance that is one of the main problems in the world.

By the time my next album, *Freedom of Speech . . . Just Watch What You Say,* came out, I had already seen just exactly how much protection the First Amendment offered black rappers in this country. I was beginning to see how worried everybody was about what I had to say.

In the song "Freedom of Speech," I rapped:

**Let me tell you about down South
where a muthafucka might as well
not even have a mouth.
Columbus, Georgia, said they lock me up
if I got on the stage
and in my show I said, Fuck.
So I thought for a minute and said, No.**

■ **All you wanna do is tell the truth.**

164

I wasn't even gonna do a damn show.
'Cause for me to change my words
From my rhymes is never gonna happen
'cause there's no sell out on mine.
But I'm vowed to get those muthafuckas one day.
They even arrested Bobby Brown and Cool J.
Yo, they got theirs coming 'cause I'm mad, and
I'm gunning homeboys and there's no running
I'm gonna tell you how I feel about you.
No bull, no lies, no slack, just straight fact.
Columbus, Georgia, you can suck my dick
you ain't nothing but a piece
of fucking shit on a damn map.

When I wrote those lines in '89, I'd been out on tours and I was running into "freedom of speech." People had already told me what I could not say onstage in Columbus, Georgia. You couldn't say anything they called a "swear" word. You couldn't touch yourself. They were using the same tactics they used on everyone from Elvis and Jim Morrison to 2 Live Crew.

The album art also reflected exactly what I had learned about free speech. The character on the cover is an average B-boy, and he has a gun in his mouth and a gun pressed up against each side of his head.

The concept of that picture is, "Go ahead and say what you want. But here comes the government and here come the parents, and they are ready to destroy you when you open your mouth." How the fuck can anybody be expected to speak when those guns are always there?

When we came out with *Original Gangster* in '91, it wasn't really considered a controversial album. At this point in my career, everything I'd spoken on prior to that had

■ All you wanna do is save the youth.

manifested itself. It was as if the public said: "Oh, we thought he was talking shit, but he kind of did tell the truth."

In addition, songs like "Let's Get Butt Naked and Fuck" had blazed a trail for other rappers to make even crazier, harder records. I never was a shock-oriented musician; I didn't intentionally reach for extremes. I was just telling it like I saw it. But now, groups like N.W.A. had totally blown the shit up, and I felt vindicated.

On April 29, 1992, just a few weeks after we dropped *Body Count,* total vindication came with the uprising. My enemies didn't even want to fuck with me anymore. We'd get phone calls asking what I thought of martial law. I'd tell them to refer to album three, track one. We'd predicted martial law.

They'd keep asking questions and finally I told them, "Listen to my records. Listen to *Body Count.*"

Body Count was intentionally different from an Ice T album. An Ice T album has intelligence, and at times it has ignorance. Sometimes it has anger, sometimes it has questions.

But *Body Count* was intended to reflect straight anger. It was supposed to be the voice of the angry brother, without answers. The tone of the record wasn't, "Why do the police hurt me? Why are parents racist?" It was, "Fuck the police. Fuck your parents."

If you took a kid and you put him in jail with a microphone and asked him how he feels, you'd get *Body Count:* "Fuck that. Fuck school. Fuck the police." You wouldn't get intelligence or compassion. You'd get raw anger.

Body Count says, "Let me put you in touch with that anger." That's how I analyzed N.W.A when they came out. Reporters would say to me, "Your music is different than N.W.A.'s. N.W.A.'s. is stupid." I would explain to them N.W.A. ain't stupid. They just didn't understand what N.W.A. means. N.W.A. is Niggas With Attitude. It's sup-

■ Ice Cube knows, Soulja knows, P.E. knows,

posed to be visceral. It's intentionally expressed with attitude.

Body Count was an angry record. It was meant to be a protest record. I put my anger in it, while lacing it with dark humor.

We decided to fuck with three enemies in *Body Count*:

THE KKK ("KKK Bitch"). The KKK is a hate organization based around genocide of anybody who is not a white Anglo-Saxon Protestant. I hate them because they would like to see me dead. I shouldn't have to explain to you why that organization would be my enemy. If you've read this far in this book and you still don't understand why I don't like the KKK, stop reading this book at this moment, put it down.

We fucked with the KKK because I feel the true fear of the white racist man is his woman leaving him for a black man and systematically eliminating the white race—i.e., the white woman making love with the black man.

"KKK Bitch" was ironic because the sentiments were true. We'd play Ku Klux Klan areas in the South and the girls would always come backstage and tell us how their brothers and fathers didn't like black folks.

"What does your father do?" I'd ask.

"He's the chief of police."

"Is he in the Ku Klux Klan?"

"Kinda."

"What are you doing here?"

"I think this is a good record. Let's get busy."

We knew that "KKK Bitch" would totally piss off the Ku Klux Klan. There's humor in the song, but it fucks with them. It's on a punk tip.

RACIST PARENTS ("Momma's Gotta Die Tonight"). Anyone who brings an innocent child into this world and decides to teach them hate is our enemy.

"Momma's Gotta Die Tonight" was written to mess with anybody who has a racist heart. It's about a kid who dis-

■ **They throw death blows.**

members his mother over racism. In the record, I play a black kid who kills his mother over a white girl. A white kid could kill his mother over a black girl, and it would be essentially the same song.

I also wanted the record to be a metaphor for the dismembering of racism, a dismembering of the whole attitude. Whoever is still perpetuating racism has got to die, not necessarily physically, but they have to kill off that part of their brain. From now on, consider it dead. The entire attitude is dead.

When we wrote the album, we thought people would trip off that record 'cause we thought people would take the sentiment literally. But obviously not.

BRUTAL POLICE ("Cop Killer"). We targeted police who feel it's not their job to solve problems, but to perpetuate them.

At the very beginning of "Cop Killer," I dedicate it to the LAPD and to police chief Daryl Gates. The lyrics are blatant and very specific; the chorus explains what the record's about:

> COP KILLER, it's better you than me.
> COP KILLER, fuck police brutality!
> COP KILLER, I know your family's grievin'
> Fuck 'em!
> COP KILLER, but tonight we get even.

Better you than me. If it's gonna be me, then *better you*. My anger is clearly aimed at *brutal* police.

People who came after the record didn't understand how I could sing, "I know your family's grieving." My response to them was, Fuck 'em. Fuck 'em. *Our* parents are grieving for the death of our kids. They've been grieving for a long time, and the number of dead cops can't even begin to com-

■ And if you got kids or a girl that's true.

pare to the number of dead kids. In 1991, three cops were killed in the entire state of California. That same year, eighty-one people in L.A. *alone* were killed by cops in *proven* police-misconduct cases.

The song was created to be a protest record—a warning, not a threat—to authority that says, "Yo, police: We're human beings. Treat us accordingly. The moment you step outside of the law, then it's fair for us to step outside of the law, too. And somebody's gonna die, and it's better you than me."

So what happened? The record is out. My fans didn't consider *Body Count* a controversial record. They listened to "Cop Killer" and smiled and understood it. My fans got a direct line on me, and they know that if I'm controversial, they are, too. You just don't hear them because they don't have a platform like I do. They're not on *Arsenio* or CNN.

The album debuted at 32 on *Billboard*'s Top 50 albums—not bad for the first hardcore rap-to-rock crossover. *Body Count* toured with Lollapalooza in the summer of '91. In twenty-one cities, 430,000 predominantly white kids waved their fists in the air and screamed "Cop Killer" along with us. Nothing happened. In the winter of 1991–1992, Body Count headlined its own tour. We hit seventy cities, performed "Cop Killer" to wild fans at about eighty shows. Nothing happened.

Then the first verdict comes in. After looking at Rodney King writhe around on asphalt for about a year, with people watching the cops go free, the shit hits the fan. Cops are now being found guilty of brutality all over the United States.

For the first time in a long time, people outside of the ghettos were looking at the cops as the actual savages and criminals that some of them really are. But honest cops were being prejudged and hurt behind this sweat. This is just how it went down.

They'll move on them, too.

169

People were glaring at the cops. The cops. The cops. The cops. The cops. "The cops started the riots. The cops killed my brother. Fuck the cops. . . ."

Out of nowhere, a cop in Houston, Texas, discovers "Cop Killer," and the record must have scared the shit out of him. "Oh shit," he figured. "They're rioting in L.A. And now, here's a record telling people to go kill the cops. Oh my God, even more frightening, it's a rock record and it's backed by Bugs Bunny's company!"

Through rock 'n' roll, I injected black rage into white kids. I have no doubt the cops were just as angry we formed a South Central rock group as they were about the song.

They said, "This muthafucka's not even doing rap. But let's call it rap in the press to make it even more incendiary." Rap immediately conjures up scary images of Black Ghetto. If they'd said it was a rock record, people might have said, "Well, okay, rock, I grew up on Fleetwood Mac. Maybe I might like it."

No, the cops knew they didn't need any sympathizers. "We need a word that conjured up niggers—Rap, yeah, black rapper. You never liked that shit."

"Rapper Ice T" created an immediate response. Rednecks quickly lined up to hate.

My message connected to that corporation was scary as shit. I was being powered by a big business—not a business run by the Japanese, they wouldn't target that, but specifically a white-owned, white-run, all-American apple-pie business.

To make matters worse for the original cop, *Body Count* was probably in the record collection of his kid. I can not imagine that cop going into a record store and buying that album. At the very least, whoever hipped him to the record had a kid who owned it.

The police group was aptly called the Fraternal Organization of Cops. We found out this "Fraternal" gang is con-

■ But when I'm gone I'm gonna need you to carry on
■ You gotta be strong

nected in with the Masons, and I wouldn't be surprised if some of the members were connected in with the Ku Klux Klan.

So, the Fraternal Organization of Cops *decides* that this record is going to be the cause of police getting killed and somebody else—possibly Ollie North, one of America's arch-villains—came to them and said it's also a good way to take the heat off the cops. They decided to go after Warner Brothers and run a big boycott. Bill Clinton—probably in an attempt to create sympathy before announcing the Gores on his ticket—Dan Quayle, and George Bush compound this propaganda campaign by coming to the "aid" of the police and attacking me.

What did it all add up to? They managed to camouflage the issue of police brutality with me. They said, "Look how terrible Ice T is! Look how terrible Warner Brothers is! America, can you believe Warner Brothers has a record out like this?"

Immediately, everybody in this country gets mad at me and says I'm terrible. And predictably, America totally forgets about the cops who are on the street hurting people.

All of a sudden I become headline news every night. They split America down the middle and the people who came in to aid me marched in defense of the First Amendment.

This isn't where I needed help. I didn't need anybody to come and say I had the right to say it. I needed people with credibility to step up and say, "Ice T not only has the right to say it, but also fuck the police! fuck the police! Who the fuck are the muthafuckin' police that they can control you like this? We're not apologizing to you cops for what YOU'VE been doing. It's time for people to get angry along with the guy who wrote 'Cop Killer.' And some of you muthafuckin' cops might end up dead!"

No one had the courage to come out and make state-

■ And fight for our salvation.
■ But there will be retaliation, soldier.

171

ments like these. Everybody just said, "Oh, Ice T and Body Count, you have the right to say it. We love you guys, really."

I tried to make it painfully clear. I said that if police were a totally legitimate organization, I might even be a cop. I never said I agreed with crime, but I am saying that when you guys stepped over the boundaries and decided you can pass judgment, then fuck you. Fuck you.

Everybody knows a lot of cops are on the job to get over inferiority complexes they've harbored since childhood. Now as police they've got a chance to go out and whip on people. They use that badge as a shield to get out their anger. When red lights start flashing in your rearview mirror, you don't say, "All right, a cop. I'm safe now." No, instead, you're fucking scared. If you're me, you know not only can they arrest you, but they might just kill you right there or throw you into a judicial system that's not equipped to treat you fairly.

Where I come from, cops never did come get your cat out of a tree. They came to collect people. If you don't believe this, you live in a state of denial. When you're sitting on a jury in Simi Valley, you believe in the myth of the American way. "The police were right. You can't lie and be a cop, can you?"

People are so mind-fucked by the myth that no matter what they see on TV or hear on the news, they refuse to believe cops are corrupt. They certainly don't believe the testimony of a black man. But if Clint Eastwood is doing the narrating, well then, that's a whole different story.

During the exact same time my record was being condemned, the film *Unforgiven* was winning critical praise across the country. What's *Unforgiven* about? A cop killer. Eastwood takes justice into his own hands after his buddy, a black man, is unjustly murdered by a corrupt cop.

What's "Cop Killer" about? A black youth takes justice into his own hands after his buddies are unjustly murdered

■ **This is a message to the soldiers.**

172

by corrupt cops. Just like Eastwood, I'm saying, *"Fuck the police,* for my dead homies," but my story is real. I know firsthand how bad the street is. America is simply not ready to hear it from me.

Now that this whole thing has blown up, I'm supposed to feel bad. I don't give a fuck about the police's problems, if I offend them or I cause them to be mad at records. They are not above scrutiny. They're not above ridicule. So now, they're mad at me. Do you think it's possible for the police to treat me worse than they've always treated me? Fuck them.

This rock 'n' roll record by "Rapper Ice T," who was waving the Time Warner flag behind him, really fucked with them. Believe me, if I could give them one night of inconvenience for the four hundred years they done fucked over my people, I was happy to do it.

Even though there were people who understood this and really were on my side, they didn't have a platform to voice their opinions. The people who did have a platform were way off backing me on the First Amendment.

That's not where all the anger should have been directed. The anger should have been generated back at the police. It was a wide-open opportunity for America to redeem itself and say, "You know what? Y'all muthafuckas better get your shit together, because y'all muthafuckas are out of pocket. I can see why a kid might want to kill you."

Okay? That's what needed to be said. Not, "Ice T has free speech." That's bullshit. Because people jumped on the wrong issue they were able to drive this thing totally through Warner Brothers.

After the cops called this embargo against Warner Brothers, they moved into criminal activity. They sent death threats to Warner Brothers. They actually sent two bombs to the label. Real bombs. These came from either the police or police sympathizers. It doesn't really make a difference: If a cop

■ **This is a message to the soldiers.**

173

sends a bomb, he is a criminal. But if these people are so down with justice, yet they would send a bomb, they're criminals, too.

It's irrelevant whether it was the police or a police sympathizer. They're supposed to be down with the law, so why are they committing a crime?

There is no way I can prove that the bombs came from police, but they did make death threats. They made death threats to the president of Warner Brothers, Lenny Waronker: "Do you know where your kids are?" Somebody went to my fifteen-year-old daughter's high school and pulled her out of class and asked her questions about me. I mean, real tacky shit.

These are the people who are supposed to be upholding justice. In effect, I had reached out and scared the guards of the system, and the system—which is made up of people who think everything is fine in this country—use the guards to protect them. When I scared their guards, the guards ran to the people and said:

"Are you gonna let him threaten us?"

"Oh, no, no, no," they cried.

"If you let him threaten us, we won't protect you anymore. Don't you want us to protect you?"

It irritated me that none of the attacks were really aimed at me. I was watching the TV and it's all Warner Brothers, Warner Brothers, Warner Brothers, Warner Brothers. You can read any paper and you'll never find anybody who said, "Where does Ice T get the anger to make the record?"

The cops never accused me of faking the anger. They knew it was real. They were just saying, "Why would you, Warner Brothers, put it on record?"

Ultimately, the guards of the system said to Time Warner, "We understand why you're mad, Ice T. But why would the big white corporation—who's a member of the same country club as us, whose kids go to spring break with our kids, who

■ **To think that rap could be attacked,**

supports the same politicians that we do—be associated with those niggers?"

And that question just rings on in my head.

"How can you be associated with that rage? We're not mad at Ice T for making the record; we know why Ice T would make that record. But why would you give him a platform, allowing him to reach the masses with that anger? I thought we were friends? You can't do that. Not if you want to be in business with us.

"Matter of fact, we may not like another record. As long as you put out records and you want to be in business with us, we're gonna have to approve it."

Warner Brothers responded that they could not afford to have the cops controlling the company, and they decided to back me. They didn't back me because they cared about me. Warner Brothers is an information company, and they cannot be told what they can or cannot do. What happens if they don't like another Ice T record? What happens if they don't like a movie Warner puts out? They were totally paranoid of paying off for the hostages, paying the extortionist.

Meanwhile, I get to the point where I am getting tired of seeing myself on the news every night. The media even got personal with me. I was tired of this shit. It wasn't worth it because nobody who had a voice was backing me on the real reason.

Ironically, 35,000 black police officers said they would not join in with any boycott of Ice T or Time Warner because they knew I was saying the truth. Since July, hundreds of cops have come up to me saying, "Ice, I know what that record is about, I'm not dumb."

I've signed more autographs this year for cops than I have in my life. "Cop Killer" totally divided the police stations. I've had cops come to me and say, "Ice, I feel like killing some of these guys I work with." Others said, "We ain't all

■ Is ignoring the simple fact,

bad." That meant a lot to me. Even the thought that they would think I'm worthy of being spoken to was cool. It was like they care that I care.

I understand a lot of cops out there are trying to do the right thing. And in a way, those cops are on the same mission I am. So it's not like they shouldn't care. I respect that.

But the other ones, fuck 'em.

As the controversy raged on, I knew I had to make a move to deal with it. I didn't want anything to happen to someone at Warner Brothers, because I knew everybody up there didn't agree with my record. In addition, it wasn't for them to fight my battle.

I didn't have any fear about something happening to somebody on the street, 'cause that's not my job. I've been putting music out on the street for years. If cops were all out there doing an honest job, people wouldn't hate them so intensely. I was more worried about some lunatic hurting somebody at Warner Brothers or even about one of those cops going out and killing a cop and trying to pin it on me.

Nobody came to me and asked me to pull the record—definitely not, no matter what muthafuckas want to say. The guys in my group didn't even know I was gonna do it. I called a meeting with Body Count and said, "This record is out of control. They are going over the top with it and ain't nobody really down with it but us. Our fans who wanted the record have already bought the album, it's gold. All the new people who are buying the record are just snooping assholes. That's not why we want to sell records. So let's pull the muthafuckin' record. The cops are arguing that we're doing it for money. So let's pull it and then tell them to shut the fuck up."

Now it's gone. Now what? In other words: Come on out and say that you just don't like Ice T. Just come on out and say it. It had become a chess game, and they shut up.

■ That they never meant for us to speak.
■ They had planned to keep the black man weak.

176

Stories about brutal police officers were starting to crop up in the press. Newspapers began running articles about new police-brutality charges. The area my stories had been taking up was now being replaced with reality.

The cops had really created fiction. "Ooh, look what this record is gonna do. This record is gonna make people kill us. This is a dangerous issue." It never was. They concocted a brilliant fictional monster: A record. And they scared the life out of people with it.

The minute I pulled it, cops killed a kid in Texas who was thirty feet away from 'em. Cops killed a kid in Detroit. People are marching: "Ice T was right." It flips now.

During this period, I also faced a backlash. After I pulled "Cop Killer," people started jumping off and saying I shouldn't have pulled the record. They said it was a sign of weakness.

I didn't give a fuck. Ice Cube told reporters on MTV, "I'm not qualified to tell Ice T what to do." Cube's basically saying, "I got respect for Ice." And Chuck D made the best comment to MTV's Kurt Loder out of everybody. He said, "Those who aren't in the war should never comment on the battle." All these people who condemned me weren't in the war.

It's so easy to pass judgment when you don't know what the fuck's going on. The people who were on the inside told me I'd made the right move. Because in a war—and make no mistake, this is a war—sometimes you have to retreat and return with superior firepower.

Even though Warner Brothers had my back, they only had my back on that issue. I didn't really feel like I had my feet placed strongly enough to hold on. So what good is holding on to that record, if I can't come back out with a record bigger and crazier than that?

I knew Warner Brothers felt they could get over the "Cop

■ But rap hit the streets—
■ Black rage amplified over dope beats.

177

Killer" incident, but there would be no reply to "Cop Killer" on my next album.

I knew where I stood. I decided I had to retreat and come back correct. I just looked around and I said, "All you mutha-fuckas ain't shit. Fuck you. I'm in this controversy by myself."

The next heated element of the controversy was pre-dictable: Did Warner Brothers ask me to pull the record? The answer to that is, No. Warner Brothers has defended artistic freedom since the beginning. Warner Brothers is the number-one hated label by the Parents Music Resource Center. They've been fighting Tipper Gore for years. They've put out everyone from Sam Kinison to Slayer, from Andrew Dice Clay to Prince and Madonna. They never shied away from con-troversial music. They put out every one of my records with-out censoring them. Dig this, they put out "Cop Killer."

But they got hit with the Establishment's vibes. The cops very wisely moved on Time Warner, which is the parent com-pany of Warner Records and twenty times bigger than the label. So they put a whole bunch of people who had no concept of art into the game by hitting their bank accounts.

Time Warner was not only attacked from the outside, they were attacked from within. The politicians and the cops managed to get Charlton Heston and people among Time Warner's shareholders to side with them. Tactical infiltration, pure and simple. It wasn't just a bunch of cops crying to the shareholders, "We don't agree."

Time Warner had people on the inside, who had never listened to my music and who had no understanding of where I was coming from, saying, "Look at what we're selling. This is our money being threatened, and I don't agree with it." Heston, who disputed my lyrics at the shareholders' meeting in '92, is probably a hired gun, hired to smear me and the company. They probably hired him. And believe me, that

■ Now they want to shut us down,
■ And they don't fuck around.

178

muthafucka probably got paid off. But then again, he's such a right-winger he probably didn't need to get paid.

I had a meeting with Lenny Waronker, and he said he felt Heston did a terrible thing at the shareholders' meeting. Lenny told me directly that Heston's attack on my music was like saying "Fuck you" in the face of all the Warner Brothers record executives. He said Heston's attack on the creative process was wrong—pure and simple.

Who the fuck is Charlton Heston, anyway? Who is he?

Lenny told me his entire career has been based around making music and putting ideas out there, and Heston comes out of nowhere and puts down his whole career.

It was some real ill shit. I know I'm fucked if I want to say something about it on the next record. Warners wouldn't come out and say I couldn't attack Heston or the cops, but you knew they were thinking it. They had Warner Brothers by the balls. The cops had won. Warner Brothers said the controversy cost them in the area of $150 million. I don't know if they ever regained that money. The police groups pulled a lot of their pension-fund money out of Time Warner stock, and they caused people to panic.

In the meantime, we go out on tour and I run into these new boycotts out on the road. These cops are threatening the club owners, saying they'll shut them down if they let us play.

People were shocked: "Goddamn, didn't they want you to pull the record? You pulled the record and now they're still fucking with you." So we came up with the conclusion that their animosity and their vendetta against me will now be for the rest of my life. They feel I threatened their life, so it's on. Fuck it. If you want to play like that, cool. I never apologized to the police, and I refuse to apologize. All I am to these muthafuckas is defiant, and that defiance bothers them more than anything else.

■ Check the history books, son,
■ Black leaders die young.

The only concession I'll make is to the honest cops who misunderstood the record and took it as a blatant attack on all police officers, which it is not. It's directed at your criminal partner, who you have to deal with. It's his record.

I ran into plenty of "criminal partners" on the road. Club owners repeatedly came up to me and said, "I never knew the cops were this criminal. I never knew it, man. Damn, the techniques they use to threaten me with . . ."

Some club owners stayed down because they got angry, others caved in. Although the tour had no violence, no problems, we had one show canceled in Pittsburgh because the cops threatened the owner. I can't get mad at the owner, because I understand this is my mission and I'm serious about it. But I can't expect other people to be as serious as I am.

I wish everybody was down. If everybody was as focused as me, then they'd really be in trouble. We'd have really solid attitudes about shit; the shit would move. We would have shut this case up once and for all. But at this moment, I'm not dealing with those types of soldiers out there.

When this tour wrapped, I knew that.

When we finished my next album, *Home Invasion,* for a November 15, 1992, release, Warner Brothers was biting its nails. Warner had the album reviewed by a "crisis attorney," an attorney who assesses potential problems, the same attorney who reviewed *The Last Temptation of Christ.*

This was the first work I'd put out since the "Cop Killer" drama. So he listens to the record and finds a few places where the album, he decides, will cause problems. References to cops here and there, which I didn't give a fuck about.

I knew they were going to ask me to change the lyrics— something they had not done before—so before they could tell me to change them, I gave them my idea. "You guys look worried. I ain't trying to get y'all in trouble. But I ain't trying

■ **They tell us that our words are scary.**

to change my record neither. So why don't we ask ourselves why they're after us? Are they after you? Are they after me? Or is it some political shit, the timing of the record's release? Let's wait till after the presidential election." Now I'm playing record executive here. "Let things cool down. We have Ice Cube's album coming out, we've got Dre's album coming out, *Paris*. You've got all the other toxic material coming out. Let's let them hit and see what happens."

Warner Brothers was off the hook, breathing easy.

So we wait and nothing happens.

Now the new release date is February 14. And I decide to put more songs on the album in the time I'm waiting. You can't let rap get stale, so each time it rolled back a month, I'd put a new song on it.

Now, the date's here and everything is cool. They haven't decided to change any of the words. We got beyond that. But they did come at me with one song that worried them: "Ricochet." The song starts out:

You go on and on and you don't stop.
You got sticky sneakers from the blood of a
shot cop

I explained to them that the record was *already* out. "Ricochet" was the title song to a movie I'd been in, with Denzel Washington and John Lithgow.

"They wouldn't fuck with that," I told them.

"They might," they said.

The Warners people weren't angry at me or my music; it was simply a paranoid reaction on their part. They had become slaves to the "chilling effect." They'd say, "We're not crazy. But there are crazy people out there who are gonna fuck with us."

I decided that "Ricochet" was already out as a sound-

■ They're revolutionary.

track single, and it had sold well. It was already an old song. Fine, I'll drop it, and I'll create new songs rather than fight over an old record that's already been out.

I'm working with them. I'm Mr. Calm. But there's always a point where you push it too far.

Although they had already approved *Home Invasion*'s cover art, we got a phone call a week before the album was scheduled to drop: "You can't have that album cover."

■ Because we speak the truth about crime and drugs,

I was still on the road, and I'm pissed. I love the album cover. But fuck it. At this point, I want my record to come out.

I told them to put the album out with a black cover. It'll be *The Black Album*. Fuck it. Just get it out there. I don't give a fuck.

But when I got back to L.A., I realized fully for the first time that Warner Brothers cannot afford to be in the business of black rage. They can be in the business of white rage, but black rage is much more sensitive. The angry black person is liable to say anything. The angry black person might just want to kill everybody. You just don't know. So, they can't be in the business of black anger while being in the business of black control, which is another part of the system.

So, we wrote them a letter asking to get out of my contract. As much as they felt I had become a liability to them, they in effect had become a liability to me. In my attempts to keep them out of trouble, my integrity had come under fire. My entire career is based on integrity. And I didn't want to be their token "free speech" employee. I didn't want them to be able to say, "We're a free speech haven because we've got Ice T, and he's radical," while they turn around and tell me what I can and cannot say. I'm not a puppet.

They gave me a release.

I know it hurt a lot of people, because Seymour Stein signed me seven years ago and watched me grow. I had sold a lot of records for him, and I would have given them four more. And now, out of nowhere, he has to release one of his main artists. Remember, I hadn't made any of them mad. They weren't mad at me, they were pissed at the entire situation. That's why I tried to stay out of the press, because the press was only looking for dirt.

We were essentially two kids who couldn't play together anymore:

■ And expose the real thugs.

183

"Okay," I said. "I'm gonna throw this rock."

"Ice, man, we got to control that rock."

"Yo, but I got to throw the rock, man. I gotta."

"Can't you just throw a pebble?"

"Nah. I got to throw a rock."

"How 'bout a smaller rock?"

"No. I got to throw this rock, because it comes from my heart. Hey, you guys want to go home?"

"Yeah. Yeah. We do."

And that's how it ended, and I understand.

Now, through Rhyme Syndicate Records, we're gonna do it ourselves. I will once again attempt to speak freely. I will have to prepare for any further attacks. Even if everybody at Time Warner had been down with me—which they weren't—are they ready to mount an offensive over the next group that attacks them?

Throughout my career, I learned that you don't talk the talk if you can't walk the walk. Don't expect to be controversial, and not suffer the ramifications of it. On my new song, "A Message to the Soldiers," I rap:

> **You might think that you're just dope,**
> **while you're living in a sniper's scope.**
> **I'm not trying to scare you,**
> **but there's danger if you get too deep.**
> **Some nights I don't sleep.**

Never underestimate what can happen to you and how hard they'll come at you.

Freedom of speech, yeah, just watch what you say . . . especially regarding my opinion of the controversy, but who gives a fuck?

> ■ **This info is not beneficial**
> ■ **To the groups that go by three initials.**

10
The Future/
No Fear

Martin Luther King, Jr., had his dream for the future of America, and I have mine. In 1963, King said: "I have a dream that one day on the red hills of Georgia the sons of former slaves and the sons of former slave owners will be able to sit down together at the table of brotherhood. I have a dream that one day even the state of Mississippi, a state sweltering with the heat of injustice, sweltering with the heat of oppression, will be transformed into an oasis of freedom and justice."

Thirty years later, those red hills of Georgia are still burning with hatred and poverty; brother and sisters from Mississippi to New York to California are still fighting for justice from an oppressive system.

My dream for this country's future would allow King's dream to come true. I want to see correct young

Isn't it sad that you put me on a pedestal 'cause I tell the truth?

■ **So they try to discredit,**
■ **They'll dog you with an edit.**

urban capitalist guerrillas band together and take this shit over. I want to see the people coming out of the ghettos and the kids coming out of college pool their resources and fight the system with capital.

What is "the system"? It isn't some vague, meaningless term. The system is the sum total of the people who feel that everything right now is A-okay. "America the beautiful. People shouldn't get welfare. Black people should stay in the ghetto, and if that's not good enough for them, go back to Africa. Keep immigrants out of the country. I don't want anybody of another race in my country club. I like things just the way they are." If you use words like "tradition" or "the good old days," you are the system.

The system is not a closed room of people who talk and make plans behind your back. It's the guy right next to you. It's the person who agrees with this tired way of thinking. Now, if you're in the system, and you want to see reform and equality go down, then you're a warrior. Some of you are reading this book and you know you can fight with me. Some of you graduating from high school or college will go into the system by becoming part of major corporations, but will always remember the injustices that were perpetrated against you growing up. Many of you should be reaching out to other people to give them a chance to fight. To do any of this, we have to have capital.

Back in the '60s, the radicals were filled with good intentions, but they had no money to back up their actions. "Oh, we're flower children, we don't need money to fight the system. Peace. Love." Get the fuck in the paddywagon. You have to have cash flow if you're gonna fight for equality. I'm about seeing rich radicals take over. That's the only way you can take over this shit. I'm about infiltrating the system to overthrow it.

■ **Print the words the way you never said it.**

186

I am not a separatist. I do not believe in just getting black people to come together. I ain't with that. I want everybody to see their opportunities. I want this whole muthafucka. I want the beach. I want the mountains. I want the whole shit, because we can do this as people, we can take this shit over, but we have to infiltrate, and we have to keep the same mindset. There are still a lot of injustices.

My vision of an urban capitalist guerrilla is the complete opposite of a yuppie. Yuppies went in and became a part of the system without any vision or any conscience. They are the people sitting behind the desks today who won't give you the bank loan you need. They forgot where they came from. Young urban capitalist guerrillas remember the injustice because their wealth is a means to an end. They remember being pulled out of their car on their way home from school by brutal police and being thrown to the ground because they "fit a description." They remember not fighting back because they didn't have the money to pay an attorney. Young urban capitalist guerrillas remember being turned down for a job because their hair was too long and being too broke to fight the employer's policy of discrimination. They remember the humiliation they suffered, and today they want to fight back.

In my definition of these warriors, I use the word capitalism because I'm trying to teach the youth—especially my black brothers and sisters—that we've all got to have money to make it happen. All of James Bond's best enemies were billionaires, right? If you're gonna take over the world, you'll need some cash.

This is no bullshit. The system attacked me this year, and if I didn't have any money, I might not still be around here now. But I have some money, and I learned the power of cash.

Empty pockets and the total lack of financial know-how

■ But we gotta make 'em regret it, soldiers.

are the main problems with the oppressed. I know we could fight back if we can get economic footing—especially black people. If we could just get our forty acres and our mule, we'd be satisfied. We'll take that in cash and distribute it through our charities and colleges and start instituting real changes. It would at least give us a foot up. You have to remember that after the Holocaust in Nazi Germany, when six million Jews were killed, at least the new German leaders took money out and gave restitution to the families who suffered the loss of their people. Fifty million blacks were killed during *our* Holocaust, and we ain't got a fuckin' dime. We ain't even got an apology yet.

Time to ante up, America. Give us our restitution. Allow us a chance to live decently and humanely. I believe America can change if we can just get things straight. Dr. King said that anybody who wants more than to be equal is ludicrous. That's all we're asking. We shouldn't have to fight for equality, but we do and will continue to.

Fear keeps so many people in this country immobilized—fear of living, fear of dying. I overcame my fear a long time ago, but you have to understand where I'm at in my life. It took me thirty-four years to understand that there are four stages of life and awareness.

At stage one, you're a child, and you don't know anything. You don't know hatred and you don't know racism or fear.

Stage two kicks in when you're a teenager and you think you know everything. You think you know black and white, right and wrong. You've figured everything out. We've all been through that stage, where we thought we knew everything and nobody could tell us different.

Stage three occurs in adulthood, when you start to learn that what you were so certain about in your younger years was probably wrong, because now as an adult, you finally "know" what's going on in the world.

Stage four is the realization you don't know anything. It's when you get back to the ability to say, "You know what? I don't know what's going to happen." It is in that adult stage of infancy where everything becomes vague and uncertain again that we can really be artistic and can reach out and attempt to learn what's going on.

Unfortunately, 99 percent of the people in this world live at stage three. They don't want to take risks because they are afraid. They are afraid of losing their jobs or losing control over their tightly confined lives.

I live my life at stage four. I look at my life like a van rolling down the street. I keep stuffing things in the front door because the back door is open and my life could be falling apart out the back, but I am continually loading up the front with new ideas and new projects. I'm continually moving. This past year, the controversy caused people to panic. I lost a TV show, I had problems with a record, a comic book fell through. People around me started to panic. But I never look back. I'm not doing that. I've learned that every time something goes wrong, if I can go around it and grab it, it usually comes back stronger.

So life is a continuous challenge for me. I've almost gotten excited about shit that ain't working. If a friend who I've loaned money to dogs me, I say to myself, "Cool, that's one less muthafucka I got to deal with. If he hadn't dogged me now, he might have been around when we got hundreds of millions of dollars, and then he could have really jerked me. So he jerked me for a thousand bucks. Good. I don't even want the money. He's gone. Let's move on."

I don't look back. I don't see what you gain by dwelling on the past and bitching about things you can't change. You have to keep moving forward.

■ **Word! I know a lot of brothers out there want to get into this war,**
■ **You know what I'm saying?**

●　　■　　■

When Ronald Reagan used to talk about the "good old days" and George Bush and Dan Quayle harped on "traditional values," they weren't appealing to me or anybody who's black. How the fuck can we be in on traditional values? The tradition of America is to own slaves. Tradition. The good old days. Oh, you mean when I was on the back of the bus? When I couldn't drink from your water fountain or eat in your restaurants?

I don't understand why people cling to this image of the good old days. All I can see is the future. And hope. So, what's behind me has to catch me 'cause I'm moving forward. So even if the police bust a U-turn on me, it doesn't matter.

A friend of mine once told me that God should put one eye in the front of our head and one eye in the back so that we can see people coming up behind us. I agree to the extent that what he's really saying is each person has to be prepared to watch his own back. I already got my back. That's why I don't walk with bodyguards. That's why I don't have security around me. I watch my back with faith. I walk through the projects of L.A., and I never worry about who might come up behind me.

When you read Malcolm X—at the very least, I hope you saw the movie—at the end of his life he didn't want any security guards around him. He chose to walk alone. Do you know why? When you get to a certain level, you realize how diabolical the enemy really is. I realize no matter how many people I've got around me, when it's time for me to go, it's coming right between the eyes and there will be nothing I can do about it.

I'm moving forward. Both of my eyes are aimed directly at the future. I say to myself, "Okay, cool, cool, cool." I'll put out my records and the minute a new record is out of my hands, I'm writing my new album. I'm so far forward,

■ A lot of sisters got a lot of knowledge they want to drop on our people.
■ But right now they're moving to shut down all hip-hop.
190

that anything that happens to me here won't affect the plans I've made for the future.

In order to advance, people have to get their eyes set to the future and stop thinking about the past. This goes for us brooding about where we came from as black people. We have to say to ourselves, "Okay, that's where I came from, but right now I'm a man and I'm here and I'm breathing. And I can make decisions in life, I can make these moves, and I can achieve. So what if they make it twice as hard. I'm twice as strong, ain't I? So it's even. And I can excel."

The worst thing that can happen to you is death, and you're gonna die anyway. So your objective should be: When are you gonna die? Are you gonna die today? Or are you gonna die twenty years from now? Right now, I could be saying to myself, "Ice T, you turned thirty-four. And you've got about fifteen more years before you're gonna be fifty. In twenty-five years, you're gonna be sixty. Fifteen years? I can think back fifteen years. Shit, I ain't got no more time," and I could start to panic. But that's not my trip. You can die tomorrow.

Death is not a big thing. After you grow up the way I grew up, you realize death is unavoidable. It's around you all the time. People are just gone. My mother's gone. My dad's gone. A lot of my buddies are gone. I never cried over a death, because I already accept death to be inevitable. I've become real hardened toward it, real cold about it. Even my little son, if he were to die—and I don't want to see him die because I want him to see some of the things I've seen—I don't think I would cry. It doesn't register to me as pain. I wouldn't want to see him catch a disease and go through life with pain. But death, that's something all of us will have to deal with one day.

So don't fear it. We know everybody's got it coming, rich or poor, black or white. You dig what I'm saying? So,

■ **The First Amendment had absolutely nothing to do with black people.**

what's the big thing about it? What's the big shit? This book will be around when I'm gone. My records will be around when I'm physically gone. Big deal. This is not a big deal.

Don't sit up and worry over the inevitable. People put far too great an emphasis on life and not enough on suffering. If you want to worry about something, worry about those who are suffering. When I see people with broken spirits or poor people living on the streets or I see those who are in agony from a disease or an addiction, that to me is pain, that's suffering. That's what we need to eliminate. Let's eliminate miserable realities.

Despite the frustration and anger I vent in my music, I have a great deal of hope for the future. When I meet with kids around the country, they all give me reason to be optimistic. I spoke at Stanford University this year, and the students continued asking me questions long after I was finished lecturing. After we left the auditorium, I talked for two more hours while the students sat crammed together on the floor of their dorm room's lobby. They wanted to know the answers they can't get from their textbooks and from the media. They wanted to know what they could do to help change society's problems. Spread out on the floor were a Minnesota farm kid, inner-city students, and kids from America's suburbs—all picking my brain to see where we could go from here. I told them, "Isn't it sad that you put me on a pedestal 'cause I tell the truth?" I told them that if we all told the truth and we communicated with each other, we'd have something to work with.

I know firsthand the price you pay for telling the truth. The system can come down on you hard, and you have to be prepared for it. You have to be prepared to be ridiculed because people are uncomfortable with too much truth. It's important to understand that there is nobody in the world

■ At the time the Constitution was written,
■ we were considered nothing but property.

192

who everybody likes. Michael Jackson: People either love him or say he's gone crazy. The pope: People like him and people take shots at him. There is no person who everyone likes. A friend told me a great Bill Cosby quote once: "There's no guaranteed way to win. But the guaranteed way to lose is to try to make everybody like you." So you pick the side that you're on, and you roll with it. This falls into one of my rules of life. To attempt to find happiness, immediately understand there is no way to make everybody like you. Don't feel so bad, though, because even within the system you will always find allies.

I can walk into Chasen's or any ritzy, arrogant restaurant, and I may be completely unwelcome as a customer, but the chef might be an ally, or a waiter or even the maître d' might whisper to me, "Man, I'm with you"—like we're the underground or something. A reporter might mumble before an interview, "I'm on your side, and I know what you're saying. My editor isn't, but fuck him."

I've flown on airplanes where a stewardess or a pilot will come up and say, without any introduction, "Yeah. I know what you mean." These are the people who you'll seek out, and you'll always find them. You will always find other people who are fighting parallel battles.

The government totally fucked up when they let me know they were listening to my words. Bush, Clinton, and Quayle blew it when they entered the battle and began condemning my message. Hell, yeah. If I were Muammar el-Qaddafi sitting in a Libyan bunker with my hands on some muthafuckin' nuclear warheads and an army at my disposal, I would expect the president to mention my name now and then. But I'm an entertainer.

When they started turning the focus of the country on me, they made me realize that I do have power. If anything,

■ The expectation of having black people speak on records
■ Never came to mind. So we gotta move.

they fucked up and let me know I'm not just a rapper, that I am somebody who they feel is a threat. Today, I can reach all the way through to them if I want to, whenever I want to. I didn't know that before they spoke up. I didn't know I could say anything the president of the United States would listen to. But now, Tipper Gore's in the White House, and I've got an even more direct line to them. Any time I want to say anything to Clinton, I'll just make a record. I may just send a whole fuckin' record of threats and demands to his punk ass.

When you become a public enemy in this country, you gain national access. It's amazing that I can sit home at night, and say, "You know what? I feel like being on CNN." One phone call later, there would be a camera crew in my house, and I would go on TV. How many people have that ability just to be national?

If I wanted, I could do a national address. Me and my buddies sit up and laugh about it. We're playing Nintendo: "Oh shit, Donald just won. Let's call CNN up and do a national broadcast." I sometimes wonder if I should have that kind of access, but why the fuck not? Charlton Heston and Ollie North are out there spreading their propaganda; why shouldn't I be countering it? If I were irresponsible about having the country's ear, you would already know about it.

One of the most intelligent articles I read on the "Cop Killer" controversy—and a lot of them were just plain stupid—was by a reporter who asked the people of the country why they were trippin' off me. Because if I was somebody who wanted to take this record and use it as a call to revolution and kill police, why didn't I jump on this platform I had created? Why wasn't I on TV spreading my propaganda? Why was I avoiding the press? Because, he determined, it's not what I wanted to do.

If I thought it was time for us to fight, then I would have

■ But believe me all the other black leaders have been silenced,
■ And most of the time it's been violent.

used the platform. But the reporter was smart. He was the only one to point out that if that was what I had wanted, it would've been handled. Right then, I would have been on TV saying, "Let's go. Let's do it."

For now, I make records. That's my job. In those records, I draw parallels to the different degrees of anger people feel on the street. I give people an opportunity to see a lot of the problems without having to go through the actual violence. I make records from an enraged brother's point of view. The cops are lucky I believe in enlightening the mind more than I believe in violence.

By tuning in, these punk cops and punk politicians gave me the fire to keep attempting to enlighten minds through my music. I will continue to do so as long as I am able, until I feel there is a better way.

It's up to you to change the system more than me. You decide what problems you want to address, and make them your mission. Everybody should have a mission that's fueled by the experience in their own hearts. In the arc of it, when you have touched the threshold—and I deal in the threshold in everything from sex to politics—you have to be prepared to handle your business with your own connections and your own people, because you will eventually be shut off from outside help. Remember: If you're fearless, you are dangerous to the system.

Once you're no longer afraid of death, you immediately become dangerous. You're playing by a different set of rules. Fear keeps you from moving forward. If you're fearless, you've got no choice but to advance, and if you're not looking back, you've only got hope in front of you.

Now, I just live and let the chips fall where they may. I now understand that I really don't have any control over my life. I'm just rolling with it. I don't know what the fuck's

■ So if you choose to get in this war, realize what you're in for.
■ But we gotta move on.

supposed to happen to me next. I just kind of live it. I don't know what's right. I'm just riding the muthafucka.

The key to life is to live it fearlessly. The people who make the biggest money, and the people who are most fly, are the people who take extreme risks.

Don't try to guide or control everything around you, just live it. Get on the muthafucka and ride it hard. It's gonna throw you, it's gonna hurt you, and it's gonna break you, but the minute you try to control it, you'll learn that it's bigger than you. It's nothing we have power over. So you just have to go with it. Once you learn to ride it, you are just so free. Prepare to fall off the edge, prepare to be hurt, prepare to get bit, but ride the muthafucka.

That's it—my opinion of the future, do you give a fuck?

Peace

Pimptionary/ Glossary

Bailing: to walk or run in an aggressive manner

Bitch: (negative connotation) a woman/man who feels the world revolves around her/him; (positive connotation) girlfriend or wife. Ex.: *I love my bitch!*

Bloods: gangs that wear the color red

Buggin': acting wild; having fun

Bust a U-turn: to make an illegal U-turn in traffic

A car (in prison terms): a group of inmates you hang out with; the group you would side with in a prison riot

Chillin': relaxing

Cool out: the request to calm down and relax. Ex.: *Cool out, man. Take it easy.*

Crack game: car insurance fraud

Crib: home

Cuz: Crip greeting, used by gangs that wear the color blue

Dis: to disrespect

Dogged: treated very low

Dope: (negative connotation) drugs; (positive connotation) very good; something so good it seems to give you a high. Ex.: *That's a dope car!*

Down: to be in someone's corner, the ultimate friend is *down* with you no matter what

Fit a description: you look like someone who committed a crime

Flavor: style

Flip: to change personality quickly

Fly: style; the ultimate street compliment. Ex.: *That girl is really fly.*

A 40: a 40-ounce beer, usually Old English or St. Ides

G's: thousands; one G is one thousand dollars

Game: being streetwise or having street smarts; slick

Gangbanging: the act of being in an active gang

Gangsta: member of a gang; also, a style of rap based on streetlife, which is very hardcore, violent and sexual

Get popped: to get caught by the police

Giving it up: showing gang hand signals

Glock: a type of handgun

Hitting 'em up: showing gang hand signals to opposite gang

Homie/homeboy: a friend from your neighborhood or school

'Hood: neighborhood

Hustling: earning money through illegal means, i.e., robbery, con games, pimping, etc.

Hype/hyped: exciting, cool

Ill: crazy, weird

It's on: "let's get it started," i.e., the fight, the crime, the love, etc.

The joint: prison

Kickin' it: sitting around, relaxing

A lick: a crime or the place of a crime

Loc/locing: short for loco: acting crazy, esp. when gang members prepare to fight

Lowrider: a car built with hydraulic lifts, which raise and lower the car

Mack: pimp; talk someone into something

Nine: a 9mm handgun

One-time: the police

Peel a cap: to shoot someone in the head; to murder with violence to the head

Penile: prison

Pimpin': the management of prostitutes; also used as a definition of a fly, cool lifestyle, which has nothing to do with prostitution

Poppin': extreme street fame; having everyone know your name

Props: respect

Pussy: vagina

A ride: a car, or, in prison terminology, the "set" you're in

Rollin': doing well, financially or otherwise

Set: a gang unit

The shit: the best

Shit talkin': talking crazy, usually lies or boasts

The shooter: a gang killer; the one who pulls the trigger

Shot caller: the person in a gang who makes the decisions; boss or leader

Smoked: killed; shot and killed

Square: someone with no street knowledge. Ex.: *You need this glossary because you are square.*

Straight up: the truth

A stretch/stretched: a long-term prison stay

Sweat/sweatin': to be nervous or to make nervous due to pressure

The system: the government

Tip: the tip of someone's dick. Ex.: *Get off my tip!*; to bother to the point where it feels like someone is hanging on your dick

Trimming: picking a lock with a nail file

Trippin': having fun or acting irrational

24/7: short for 24 hours a day, 7 days a week; constantly

Vibing: feeling someone's energy

Wannabe: someone trying to act real; faking

Wack: terrible

Word: true

ICE T FAN CLUB
1283 La Brea Avenue
P.O. Box 211
Los Angeles, CA 90019